LAW OF THE LAND

A Practical Legal Guide for Tourists and Business Travelers

South Africa

By Michael L. Moore Esq.

Author: Michael L. Moore

Edited by Ally Knez-Siddique

Cover Design: Kristina Conatser

Published by: Law of the Land Publishing, LLC

ISBN: 978-1-964870-17-5

DEDICATION

This book is dedicated to the memory of my late older brother, Kenneth Lee Moore, whose tragic murder at 15 years of age inspired me to write this series of books.

This book is also dedicated to my parents, John Henry Moore, and Edna Mae Moore, whose tremendous parenting skills kept me focused on the important things in life: being reverent, getting educated, and prioritizing family.

Finally, this book is dedicated to my beautiful family, my wife, my son, and my daughter. They inspire me every single day to be kind, patient, and compassionate.

IN LOVING MEMORY OF:

Belinda Joyce Moore Moss—my beautiful and wonderful sister, who supported me in every positive thing that I ever attempted to do.

Michael Eugene Baker—my dedicated and loyal friend and brother, who always wanted the very best for me.

Sylvia Joyce Hill—my eldest sister, who had a beautiful spirit and was like a second mother to me.

PREFACE

My introduction to the justice system came when I was only 10 years old. My 15-year-old brother was murdered with a butcher knife by a 19-year-old in a simple argument over a torn shirt. I was devastated by his death and sought retribution for his fate that never came. The woman was initially charged with second degree murder, but after plea negotiations, she was convicted of manslaughter and sentenced to only five years in a youthful offender school and ordered to undergo psychiatric care. That was it. Nothing more. The judicial system had run its course.

My family knew nothing about the justice system, and we did not have the tools to advocate for ourselves. No one provided us with a written source to reference for guidance through this process. There was no easily accessible, easy to understand, definitive source to educate ourselves about the legal system that we suddenly and unexpectedly found ourselves immersed in after being victimized by such a violent criminal act.

As I got older, finished college, law school, and ultimately started practicing law, it became clear to me that most people are not knowledgeable about the law or how the judicial process works. If most people are uninformed here in the United States regarding the law and the legal process, how would they fare when in other countries? I realized that tourists and businesspeople who travel internationally needed access to information on how to navigate the legal system in other countries!

For many years, there has been considerable media attention focused on international travelers experiencing legal difficulties while traveling abroad. Most of these news stories gained attention in the United States and abroad because they involved American citizens facing punishment that was considered "unconventional" and "harsh" by United States' legal standards. I recall a news story in 1994 regarding Michael Fay, a young American male, who had broken the law in Singapore. He was convicted and sentenced to be caned and or whipped publicly. While the United States Government weighed in on the inappropriate and cruel nature of the punishment, the young American was beaten because he had been convicted under Singapore law.

Similarly, in recent years, international news stories have garnered headlines regarding foreign travelers and their issues with the laws of countries that were not their own. Amanda Knox, an American woman, was accused of murdering her roommate in Italy in 2007 and spent almost four years in an Italian prison before being definitively acquitted by the Supreme Court of Cassatio. Kenneth Bae, an American citizen, was arrested in North Korea in 2012 and was convicted for hostile acts against the communist country. He was sentenced to 15 years hard labor but was released in 2014 after efforts by the U.S. State Department. More recently, United States Basketball Star, Brittany Griner was arrested in February 2022 at a Moscow airport on drug-related charges and detained for nearly 10 months, spending much of that time in prison. Her plight unfolded at the same time Russia invaded Ukraine and further heightened tensions between Russia and the United States, ending only after she was freed in exchange for a notorious Russian arms dealer.

It was in 1994 that another personal tragic event occurred that finally inspired me to write these series of books. A dear friend and also client of mine was brutally murdered while on his second honeymoon in Jamaica. News of his murder shocked me and our local community. The legal hurdles his family had to overcome to see that justice was properly dispensed far away from home, in another country, with an entirely different set of criminal procedural rules and laws, was difficult to navigate.

As I was my friend's attorney at the time of his death, his family asked that I act as their "legal liaison" to the Jamaican Prosecutor's Office and to the Jamaican Police Department. I participated in multiple police interviews with my client's widow because she was the primary witness to his murder. As a former prosecuting attorney, I was also allowed by the Court, as a professional courtesy, to sit at the prosecutor's table to consult with the prosecuting attorney during trial. What I observed about the Jamaican trial process from a front row seat was compelling enough to cause me to seriously consider educating the "world" regarding what to expect and how to act appropriately when faced with legal issues while traveling abroad.

One of the realities in life is that, regardless of what country you are in, it is never a pleasant experience to run afoul of the law and be forced to accept that someone else will be making a decision about your pecuniary, proprietary, or penal interests (your money, your property, or your freedom).

It is important to know what the laws are, how they apply to you, and how to navigate the legal system if you are charged with a crime. It is also very helpful to know what resources are available to you if you are the victim of a criminal act. At the end of the day, an "ounce of prevention is worth a pound of cure," so the more knowledge you have, the more ammunition you possess, and the more likely you will have a positive outcome.

If you are traveling to South Africa, the first thing you should pack is a copy of this book! The helpful information and tips contained in this volume will provide a great starting point for knowing what to do (and not to do!) when you arrive at your destination and will help ensure that you have a wonderful vacation or business trip unmarred by tangles with the law.

TABLE OF CONTENTS

Introduction 11

CHAPTER 1: About South Africa 19

CHAPTER 2: Customs 33

CHAPTER 3: Crime in South Africa 41

CHAPTER 4: Criminal Law Violations. 49

CHAPTER 5: Alcohol-Related Offenses 59

CHAPTER 6: Firearm & Ammunition Offenses 67

CHAPTER 7: Prostitution 77

CHAPTER 8: LGBTQ 87

CHAPTER 9: Sexually Motivated/Violent Crimes 97

CHAPTER 10: Arrested in South Africa. 105

CHAPTER 11: Jails vs. Prisons: Conditions & Culture 119

CHAPTER 12: Helping a Friend or Relative Imprisoned in South Africa 127

CHAPTER 13: The Administration of Justice 135

CHAPTER 14: Crime Victim Assistance. 143

CHAPTER 15: Police 153

CHAPTER 16: How to Get Legal Help in South Africa 163

CHAPTER 17: Medical Facilities & Hospitals 171

CHAPTER 18: Driving in South Africa. 179

CHAPTER 19: Nude Beaches & Clothing-Optional Resorts. 187
CHAPTER 20: Unusual Laws. 195
CHAPTER 21: Traveling Safely 201
CHAPTER 22: Tourist Taxation. 211
CHAPTER 23: Long-Term Stays 217
CHAPTER 24: Civil Litigation 229
CHAPTER 25: Other Things to Know 243
CHAPTER 26: Quick Reference Guide 251
Emergency/Important Contact Numbers in South Africa. 265
Useful isiZulu, Xhosa, and Afrikaans Phrases 267
Glossary 275
Acknowledgments. 279
About the Author 281

INTRODUCTION

IN THIS CHAPTER

- About This Book
- Hypotheticals Used Throughout This Book
- How This Book is Organized
- Icons Used in This Book
- Where to Go From Here

INTRODUCTION

As a practicing attorney for over 34 years, I have encountered numerous clients who travel often, but are unaware of the laws of the land they are traveling to.

Therefore, many years ago, I decided to write a series of books that would explain the laws of specific countries. My focus was to explain the laws that may affect travelers in a straightforward manner, without all of the legal language that is sometimes hard for even seasoned attorneys to understand.

About This Book

The aim of this book is simple. It provides you, the traveler, with a simple, easy to read book that will provide a basic legal guide that explains the law in the country that you are about to visit. It is not intended to educate you on ALL of the laws in a given country. The goal is to provide you with the details of the most common legal and safety issues faced by tourists and business travelers.

I have also provided context with background information on places not to visit, statistics on the country and prevention measures you should take to safeguard your legal and physical safety. Knowledge is a powerful thing and knowing how to stay out of trouble (or how to get out of it!) is important for everyone who travels.

This *Law of The Land/South Africa* book simply helps you become more informed about your legal rights, responsibilities, and obligations in a wide range of subject areas.

Last, but not least, this book does NOT purport to offer legal advice. It does, however, provide the information you need to stay safe, follow the law and navigate around legal difficulties. However, if you do face legal difficulties, the information in this book will provide you with a starting point for solving the problem and obtaining legal assistance should it be required.

Hypotheticals Used Throughout This Book

From time to time throughout this book, I will explain the law to readers by using hypothetical scenarios. These hypotheticals will be marked by an icon that will be explained in further detail as you read on.

How This Book is Organized

CHAPTER 1: **About South Africa.** This chapter will provide you with a brief overview about South Africa and its history. It also addresses Visa requirements, monetary advice, and the best times to visit.

CHAPTER 2: **Customs.** This chapter will provide information on what to expect when entering South Africa. It will also explain what restricted and prohibited items are when entering South Africa along with custom's regulations.

CHAPTER 3: **Crime in South Africa.** This chapter provides an overview of the history of crime in South Africa and steps that South African officials have taken to curb the high rate of crime.

CHAPTER 4: **Criminal Law Violations.** This chapter will provide information on drug offenses, penalties, true events and questions and answers.

CHAPTER 5: **Alcohol-Related Offenses.** This chapter will provide key points regarding the sale, consumption, and regulations of alcohol use in South Africa.

CHAPTER 6: **Firearm & Ammunition Offenses.** This chapter will provide key points regarding the possession of firearms and ammunition in South Africa.

CHAPTER 7: **Prostitution.** This chapter provides an overview of the history of prostitution in South Africa, laws and penalties, prostitution practices, sex trafficking, sex tourism, health in South Africa, tips to avoid being hassled, a Law of the Land Hypothetical, and the current situation on prostitution in South Africa.

CHAPTER 8: **LGBTQ.** This chapter will provide information regarding the acceptance of LGBTQ people in South Africa and the laws surrounding homosexuality.

CHAPTER 9: **Sexually Motivated/Violent Crimes.** This chapter will provide an overview of sexually related crimes in South Africa.

CHAPTER 10: **Arrested in South Africa.** This chapter will provide information on what to do if you are arrested in South Africa.

CHAPTER 11: **Jails vs. Prisons: Conditions & Culture.** This chapter will provide information on the conditions and culture of South African Jails and Prisons.

CHAPTER 12: **Helping a Friend or Relative Imprisoned in South Africa.** This chapter will provide information on how you can assist a friend or relative imprisoned in South Africa.

CHAPTER 13: **The Administration of Justice.** This chapter will provide information on South Africa's Legal System.

CHAPTER 14: **Crime Victim Assistance.** This chapter will provide information on crime victim assistance along with providing safety tips.

CHAPTER 15: **Police.** This chapter will provide information on the South African Police and how to report a crime.

CHAPTER 16: **How to Get Legal Help in South Africa.** This chapter will provide information regarding how to obtain legal assistance for travelers to South Africa.

CHAPTER 17: **Medical Facilities & Hospitals.** This chapter will provide information about how to obtain medical care while visiting South Africa.

CHAPTER 18: **Driving in South Africa.** This chapter will provide information on driving in South Africa, it's traffic rules, and road safety tips.

CHAPTER 19: **Nude Beaches & Clothing-Optional Resorts.** This chapter will provide an overview of nude beaches and clothing-optional resorts in South Africa, and the legality and safety of visiting nude beaches in South Africa.

CHAPTER 20: **Unusual Laws.** This chapter will provide information on some Unusual Laws in South Africa, and penalties and fines.

CHAPTER 21: **Traveling Safely.** This chapter will provide information on women traveling alone, crime prevention for families, safety notes for all travelers, and overall advice.

CHAPTER 22: **Tourist Taxation.** This chapter will provide information on taxes that tourists are required to pay in South Africa.

CHAPTER 23: **Long-Term Stays.** This chapter will provide an overview of the consequences for overstaying your visit to South Africa.

CHAPTER 24: **Civil Litigation.** This chapter will provide information about the civil litigation process in South Africa.

CHAPTER 25: **Other Things to Know.** This chapter will provide information on the harassment of tourists, travel and safety, and other practical tips.

CHAPTER 26: **Quick Reference Guide.** This chapter is a quick way to get information. It is a condensed version of the chapters in this book.

Emergency/Important Contact Numbers in South Africa

Useful isiZulu, Xhosa, and Afrikaans Phrases

Glossary

Icons Used in this Book

What do those pictures throughout the book mean? See below:

WARNING: This icon flags information about things you should **avoid** while visiting South Africa. Heed the advice next to this icon to avoid legal perils.

REMEMBER: This icon flags noteworthy information that you **shouldn't forget.**

HELPFUL TIPS: This icon flags information that will help you when entering South Africa, relates to a legal situation, or refers to resources available while visiting South Africa.

TECHNICAL INFORMATION: This icon flags technical aspects of the law. If you are faced with a legal problem, and you want to learn more about the law involved, this information can be helpful.

ADDITIONAL INFORMATION: This icon points to the location of additional information available on the internet.

HYPOTHETICAL: This icon points to hypothetical scenarios to illustrate possible legal problems and the outcome.

QUESTIONS: This icon points to questions and answers throughout the book.

TRUE STORY: This icon points to true events throughout the book.

Where to Go From Here

If you have a specific question about the law in South Africa as it relates to a particular area, just turn to the chapter that addresses that issue, or turn to the Quick Reference Guide. You can also read the book from cover to cover to obtain a more comprehensive understanding of South African laws and resources available should you find yourself in a legal predicament while visiting.

Disclaimer: While the recommendations in this book primarily address U.S. citizens, the information is relevant and applicable to citizens of any country.

CHAPTER 1

ABOUT SOUTH AFRICA

IN THIS CHAPTER

- About South Africa
- South Africa, the Basics
- South African Hospitality

CHAPTER 1

ABOUT SOUTH AFRICA

About South Africa

South Africa occupies the **southernmost part of Africa**, sharing borders with Namibia, Botswana, Zimbabwe, Mozambique, and Eswatini, and entirely surrounding Lesotho. The country spans approximately **1,220,813 square kilometers (471,359 square miles)**, making it the **25th largest nation globally**. As of the 2022 census, South Africa's population stood at **62 million**, reflecting a significant increase from 51.7 million in 2011.[1]

Historically, South Africa has been inhabited by humans for over 100,000 years, with the earliest known peoples being the San and Khoikhoi, collectively referred to as the Khoisan. Around the 4th century AD, Bantu-speaking communities began migrating into the region, bringing ironworking and new agricultural practices. European colonial presence began in 1652 with the arrival of Dutch settlers at what is now Cape Town. In the 19th century, British forces seized control, which triggered conflicts with both indigenous African kingdoms and the descendants of Dutch settlers, known as Afrikaners or Boers. These tensions culminated in the South African (Boer) War, which ended with British dominance and the formation of the Union of South Africa in 1910.

1 https://www.statssa.gov.za/?p=16716&utm

South Africa's modern history is shaped profoundly by **apartheid, a legalized system of racial segregation imposed by the white minority government** from 1948 to 1994. The system restricted rights and access to opportunities for the Black majority and other non-white populations. After decades of resistance from figures like **Nelson Mandela** and **Desmond Tutu**, along with international sanctions and grassroots activism, apartheid was dismantled. In 1994, South Africa held its first multiracial democratic elections, with Nelson Mandela elected as the first Black president. Since then, the country has made significant strides in rebuilding its institutions, promoting human rights, and fostering reconciliation, although it continues to grapple with inequality and economic disparity.[2]

The Capital

Uniquely, South Africa has **three capital cities**, each serving a distinct function. **Pretoria**, located in Gauteng Province, is the administrative capital where the President and most government ministries are based. **Cape Town**, in the Western Cape, serves as the legislative capital and is home to Parliament. **Bloemfontein**, in the Free State, holds the judiciary and is the seat of the Supreme Court of Appeal. This tri-capital system reflects the country's efforts to distribute governmental power across different regions following its unification in the early 20th century.[3]

The People

The people of South Africa are **exceptionally diverse**, which is why the country is often called the "**Rainbow Nation**." According to the 2022 census, about 81.4% of the population identifies as Black African, 8.2% as Colored (a term used in South Africa to describe people of mixed ethnic origin), 7.3% as White, and 2.7% as Indian or Asian.[4]

2 https://en.wikipedia.org/wiki/History_of_South_Africa?utm_source

3 https://www.thoughtco.com/why-does-south-africa-have-three-capitals-4071907?utm_source

4 https://en.wikipedia.org/wiki/Ethnic_groups_in_South_Africa?utm_source

This diversity stems from centuries of migration, colonialism, and cultural exchange. South Africans have a strong sense of community, with many people deeply connected to their cultural heritage, whether expressed through traditional music, clothing, languages, or religious practices. While social challenges persist, especially those rooted in the legacies of apartheid, the people of South Africa are often characterized by their resilience, warmth, and shared sense of identity.

Language

Linguistically, South Africa is one of the most **multilingual** countries in the world, with **12 official languages** recognized by its constitution. These include **Afrikaans, English, isiNdebele, isiXhosa, isiZulu, Sepedi** (Northern Sotho), **Sesotho** (Southern Sotho), **Setswana, siSwati, Tshivenda, Xitsonga,** and most recently, **South African Sign Language**, which was granted official status in 2023. The most widely spoken first language is isiZulu, accounting for 24.4% of the population, followed by isiXhosa (16.6%), and Afrikaans (10.6%). English, although only spoken at home by 8.7% of the population, plays a central role in business, politics, and education, and is commonly used as a lingua franca in urban areas and public life.[5]

Religion

Religion in South Africa reflects both its indigenous heritage and its colonial history. **Christianity is the dominant faith**, adhered to by approximately 85.3% of the population. The largest denominations include Protestant branches like Zionist and Pentecostal churches, as well as Roman Catholicism and the Dutch Reformed Church. In addition to Christianity, around 7.8% of the population practices **traditional African religions**, which often blend ancestral worship with Christian elements. Other religious groups include **Muslims** (1.6%), **Hindus** (1.1%), and a **small Jewish community**, with about 3.1% identifying

5 https://en.wikipedia.org/wiki/Languages_of_South_Africa?utm_source

as **non-religious.**[6] The South African constitution guarantees religious freedom, fostering a society in which multiple beliefs coexist peacefully.

Affordability

South Africa is widely regarded as an **affordable destination**, especially for travelers coming from countries with stronger currencies such as the United States, United Kingdom, or the European Union. The favorable exchange rate makes it possible to enjoy high-quality services and experiences at a fraction of what they might cost in more developed nations. The local currency, the **South African rand (R)**, often offers strong value against major international currencies. As of early 2025, the exchange rate averages around **R19 to R1 USD**, though it can fluctuate.

Accommodation costs cater to all budget levels. Budget travelers can find hostels or guesthouses in urban areas or backpacker-friendly towns for as little as **R250– R400 per night ($13–$21 USD)**, while mid-range hotels and B&Bs often charge between **R700 and R1,500 ($37–$79 USD)** per night. Luxury lodges and boutique hotels, especially in safari regions or along the Cape coastline, can cost upwards of **R3,000 ($158 USD)** per night, but offer world-class amenities and often include meals, guides, or game drives.

Dining out is similarly reasonable. A meal at a casual local restaurant might cost around **R120–R200 ($6–$11 USD)**, while a three-course dinner at a more upscale establishment could be around **R400–R600 ($21–$32)** per person. South Africa is known for its excellent and affordable wine, with a good bottle from a local vineyard available at supermarkets for **R70–R120 ($4–$6)**.

Transportation is efficient and budget friendly. Domestic flights between major cities like Johannesburg, Cape Town, and Durban often range from **R800 to R1,500 ($42–$79 USD)** if booked in advance. Long-distance buses, such as those operated by Greyhound or Intercape, offer routes between cities for **R300–R600 ($16–$32 USD)**, and local

6 https://en.wikipedia.org/wiki/Religion_in_South_Africa?utm_source=chatgpt.com

minibus taxis or rideshare apps like Bolt and Uber are widely available in urban areas.

Tours and activities are competitively priced. A full-day guided safari in a private game reserve may cost between **R1,800 and R3,500** (**$95–$185 USD**), while entrance to national parks like Kruger is around **R440** per day (**$23 USD**) for foreign visitors. Wine tastings in Stellenbosch or Franschhoek typically cost **R60–R120** (**$3–$6 USD**) per estate.

South Africa, the Basics

South Africa is one of the most accessible destinations in sub-Saharan Africa, with well-developed air connections to major cities across Europe, North America, the Middle East, and Asia. It is served by **several international airports**, the most prominent being **O. R. Tambo International Airport** (**JNB**) in Johannesburg, **Cape Town International Airport** (**CPT**), and **King Shaka International Airport** (**DUR**) in Durban. These hubs accommodate numerous direct and connecting flights from global cities, making travel to South Africa convenient for both short-term tourists and long-haul travelers.

O. R. Tambo International in Johannesburg is the country's largest and busiest airport, functioning as the main entry point for most international travelers. It handles flights from major carriers including **British Airways, Emirates, Qatar Airways, Lufthansa, Air France,** and **Delta Air Lines.** Cape Town International Airport is South Africa's second busiest and a popular arrival point for tourists headed to the Western Cape. It receives seasonal and year-round flights from key destinations like London, Amsterdam, Frankfurt, and Doha. Durban's King Shaka International primarily serves regional traffic but has increasing international connections, especially to and from the Middle East and southern Africa.

Direct flights from the United States are limited but available. **Delta** operates non-stop service from Atlanta to Johannesburg and Cape Town, and **United Airlines** flies direct from Newark to Cape Town. Travelers from North America can also connect through European hubs like

London, Paris, Amsterdam, or Frankfurt, which offer daily service to South African cities. Middle Eastern airlines such as **Emirates, Qatar Airways,** and **Etihad** provide popular connecting routes with one stop in Dubai, Doha, or Abu Dhabi, offering flexible schedules and often competitive prices. From Asia, airlines like **Singapore Airlines** and **Cathay Pacific** offer connecting flights through their respective hubs.

South Africa is also well-served by regional carriers and budget airlines for those traveling from within Africa. Local airline options like **FlySafair, Airlink,** and **Lift** provide affordable domestic flights and regional links. This extensive network allows travelers to enter the country easily and then move between major cities or tourist destinations such as Kruger National Park, the Garden Route, or the Drakensberg Mountains.

When to Visit?

South Africa is a year-round destination, thanks to its varied geography and climate, but the best time to visit depends on the region and the type of experience you're seeking. The country lies in the Southern Hemisphere, so its seasons are opposite those of Europe and North America. Summer runs from November to March, while winter spans June to August. Each season offers something unique, from beach holidays and safaris to cultural festivals and whale watching.

For general sightseeing, particularly in Cape Town and the Garden Route, the best time to visit is during the South African summer (**November to March**), when temperatures are warm and the days are long and sunny. This is also prime time for beach activities, hiking, and enjoying the country's rich outdoor lifestyle. However, summer can bring crowds, particularly over the December holidays, when both international and domestic tourism peaks.

For wildlife enthusiasts, winter (**May to September**) is ideal for game viewing in Kruger National Park and other reserves. During this dry season, vegetation is thinner and animals congregate around waterholes, making them easier to spot. Temperatures are cooler and more comfortable for safaris, and the risk of malaria in low-risk areas is also reduced.

The **shoulder seasons—April to May** and **September to October**—offer a great balance of good weather, fewer tourists, and often lower prices on accommodation and tours. These months are also excellent for whale watching along the southern coast, especially near Hermanus, where southern right whales migrate close to shore between June and November.

Festival lovers will enjoy South Africa's cultural calendar, which includes events like the **Cape Town International Jazz Festival** in **March**, the **National Arts Festival in Makhanda** (**June/July**), and **Durban's July horse racing event**. The country also observes a wide range of public holidays and local celebrations, reflecting its multicultural society.

Do I Need a Visa?

Whether you need a visa to enter South Africa depends on your nationality and the purpose and length of your visit. Citizens of over 90 countries, can enter South Africa **visa-free for short visits of up to 90 days for tourism or business purposes.** Travelers from countries not exempt from visa requirements must apply for a **visitor visa** in advance at a South African embassy or consulate.

South Africa is also in the process of expanding its **electronic visa (eVisa)** system, which streamlines the application process for eligible visitors. As of 2025, nationals from several countries—including Kenya, China, and India—can apply for an eVisa online without visiting a consulate, making entry more convenient.

For longer stays, such as work, study, or residency, travelers must apply for a **long-term visa or permit**, which involves more extensive documentation, background checks, and approval through South Africa's Department of Home Affairs. These applications can take several weeks to process and should be initiated well in advance of travel. (See Chapter 23: *Long-Term Stays*) It's important to note that immigration policies can change, so travelers should always check the official website of the Department of Home Affairs[7] or consult with the nearest South African embassy to confirm the latest visa requirements before planning their trip.

How to Get Around

South Africa offers a variety of transportation options for tourists, each suited to different needs, budgets, and travel styles. While the country does not have an extensive public transport system like some European destinations, getting around is still relatively straightforward, especially with a bit of planning.

For many tourists, **renting a car** is the most convenient and flexible way to explore South Africa, particularly if you plan to visit rural areas, game reserves, or the scenic Garden Route. South African roads are generally well-maintained, especially major highways and routes between cities. Car rental prices are competitive, starting at around **R400–R600 per day ($21-$32 USD)**, and fuel prices remain moderate. Tourists should note that driving is on the **left-hand side** of the road, and international drivers' licenses are generally accepted.

In major cities like Cape Town, Johannesburg, and Durban, **rideshare services** such as **Uber** and **Bolt** are widely used, affordable, and considered safe. A short city ride might cost around **R50–R100 ($3–$5 USD)**, making them ideal for quick trips to restaurants, shopping areas, or local attractions without worrying about parking or navigating.

For intercity travel, **domestic flights** are a practical option, especially considering the size of the country. Airlines like **FlySafair**, **Airlink**, and **Lift** operate regular and reasonably priced flights between popular destinations such as Johannesburg, Cape Town, Durban, and Port Elizabeth. Booking in advance often yields prices between **R800–R1,500 ($42–$79 USD)**, and flight durations rarely exceed two hours.

7 https://www.dha.gov.za/

Another viable option for intercity transport is **long-distance buses**, including services from companies like **Intercape**, **Greyhound**, and **Citiliner**. These are budget-friendly and relatively comfortable, offering routes across all major cities and towns. A typical long-distance ticket can range from **R300 to R600** (**$16–$32 USD**) depending on the distance and time of travel. **Minibus taxis**—the most commonly used form of public transportation by locals—operate widely across urban and rural South Africa. However, they are **not recommended for tourists** unfamiliar with local routes or customs, as they do not follow formal timetables or fixed stops and can be difficult to navigate without local knowledge.

Trains are available but less commonly used by tourists, with the exception of luxury services. The **Gautrain**, a modern rapid-rail link between Johannesburg, Pretoria, and O.R. Tambo International Airport, is clean, fast, and safe, ideal for airport transfers or commuting between key business hubs. For luxury travelers, the **Blue Train** and **Rovos Rail** offer high-end, multi-day train journeys through scenic parts of the country, with prices starting from several thousand rand per trip.

Monetary Advice

South Africa's national currency is the **South African Rand** (**R**), symbolized as **R.** It is subdivided into 100 cents, and commonly used denominations include R10, R20, R50, R100, and R200 notes. As of May 2025, the exchange rate hovers around **R18.50 to the US dollar**, though rates can fluctuate slightly depending on economic conditions and your exchange method. Currency can be exchanged at banks, exchange bureaus, and international airports, though using **ATMs is often the most convenient and cost-effective way** to access local money at a fair rate.

Credit and debit cards—particularly **Visa and Mastercard**—are widely accepted in cities, hotels, restaurants, supermarkets, and larger shops. **American Express and Diners Club** cards are less commonly accepted, especially outside major urban centers. It's still wise to **carry**

some cash for use in smaller towns, local markets, and for services such as tipping or paying for parking, where card facilities may not be available.

While the **US dollar, euro, or British pound** may be accepted at a few tourist lodges or upscale establishments, foreign currencies are **not used in general commerce.** It's best to convert your money into rands, as using foreign currency can result in unfavorable exchange rates or added fees. Mobile payments, such as **SnapScan and Zapper,** are increasingly popular in urban areas, especially at trendy cafes and boutique stores.

Bargaining is not a standard practice in South African retail shops, supermarkets, or restaurants, where prices are fixed. However, it is **common and often expected at informal markets, roadside stalls, and craft fairs.** When bargaining, it's important to be friendly and respectful—vendors are usually open to negotiation, but a fair approach goes a long way. Don't push too hard; if a seller isn't budging, it's acceptable to politely walk away.

Tipping is customary in South Africa and forms an important part of the income for service workers. In **restaurants,** a **10% to 15% tip** is standard and often not included in the bill. For exceptional service, tipping up to 20% is appreciated. **Hotel porters** typically receive **R10–R20 per bag** ($0.50–$1.10 USD), and **housekeeping staff** may be tipped **R50–R100** ($2.70–$5.40 USD) for longer stays. In parking lots and at informal stops, **car guards** often assist drivers and are usually tipped around **R5–R10** ($0.25–$0.55 USD). For **guided tours** or **safari drives,** a tip of **R100–R300** ($5.40–$16.20 USD) per day per person is appropriate, depending on the level of service.

South African Hospitality

South Africa is known for its **warmth, openness, and deeply rooted spirit of ubuntu,** a Nguni Bantu concept meaning "I am because we are." This idea reflects a collective sense of humanity and compassion, and it's central to how South Africans relate to one another and to guests. The country is celebrated not just for its breathtaking landscapes and wildlife, but for the friendliness of its people across its many cultural groups. Whether you're in a township, a coastal village, or a bustling city, you're likely to be greeted with genuine warmth and often treated like part of the community.

Hospitality in South Africa is typically **expressed through generosity, food, and conversation.** Visitors are often welcomed with offers of tea, coffee, or a home-cooked meal, especially in more rural or traditional settings. South Africans are proud of their diverse cuisine—from braais (barbecues) to bunny chow to traditional African stews—and sharing food is considered an important act of friendship and inclusion. Many locals will go out of their way to make visitors feel comfortable, help with directions, or engage in conversation about culture and history.

Politeness in South Africa is tied closely to **respectful greetings and body language.** It's common and appreciated to greet people with a smile, make eye contact, and say "hello" or "how are you?" even when entering a shop or service venue. In more traditional communities, especially among older people, showing respect may include addressing someone as "sir" or "ma'am," or using respectful terms in local languages (like *mkhulu* for an elder man or *gogo* for an elder woman in Zulu). Shaking hands is customary, sometimes followed by a light pat on the back or a unique regional handshake, especially among friends.

What's considered **impolite** includes not greeting people, being overly blunt, dismissive body language, or showing impatience—especially in areas where service may move at a slower pace than in Western countries. It's also frowned upon to **take photos of people, especially in townships or rural communities, without asking.** Public criticism of the country's cultural practices, even in jest, may come off as offensive, particularly given the country's sensitive history.

As a visitor, **showing respect to South African culture means embracing its diversity.** The country is home to 11 official languages and a mix of cultures including Zulu, Xhosa, Sotho, Tswana, Afrikaans, and Indian and European heritage. Making an effort to learn a few local words—like *sawubona* ("hello" in Zulu) or *dankie* ("thank you" in Afrikaans)—goes a long way in building goodwill. Being curious rather than judgmental, engaging with local guides or artisans, and supporting local businesses are all seen as signs of respect. Dressing modestly in traditional or rural areas, asking before entering private spaces, and being sensitive to the legacy of apartheid in conversations are also important ways to show cultural awareness.

CHAPTER 2

CUSTOMS

IN THIS CHAPTER

- Travelers Entering South Africa
- Customs Entitlements and Monetary Restrictions
- Restricted and Prohibited Items
- Five Practical Tips to Know Before You Go

CHAPTER 2

CUSTOMS

Travelers Entering South Africa

To enter South Africa, most travelers will need a **valid passport**, with at least two blank pages and valid for **at least 30 days beyond the intended date of departure**. Many nationalities, including citizens of the United States, Canada, most EU countries, Australia, and New Zealand, **do not need a visa for stays of up to 90 days** for tourism or business purposes. However, travelers from countries that are **not visa-exempt** must apply in advance for a tourist visa through the South African mission in their home country. The cost for a visitor visa is typically **R425** (**about $22 USD**) but can vary by country of origin.

All travelers must also provide **proof of onward or return travel** and may be asked to show evidence of sufficient funds for their stay. While proof of vaccination for COVID-19 is no longer required as of mid-2023, it's recommended to check for updates close to your departure date.

If you're traveling with **children under 18**, South Africa previously had strict documentation requirements for minors, including unabridged birth certificates. While these rules have been relaxed for many nationalities, **parents are still advised to carry birth certificates or legal documents showing parental rights or guardianship** in case they are requested by immigration officials.

For official entry requirements and visa exemptions by nationality, visit the **Department of Home Affairs** at **https://www.dha.gov.za/index.php/immigration-services/exempt-countries.**

When you land in South Africa, you'll go through a fairly standard immigration and customs process. However, there are a few South Africa-specific considerations:

- Customs regulations are strict about bringing in animal products, plants, and certain medications. You should declare anything that might fall under restricted or controlled categories.
- There are **random checks for undeclared cash**, especially amounts exceeding **R25,000 (approx. $1,300 USD)** or the equivalent in foreign currency. It's advisable to declare large amounts of money at customs.
- Baggage theft at some airports has been reported in the past, so it's wise to use luggage locks and avoid checking valuables.
- Taxis and transport services outside the airport vary in reliability; it's best to use official airport taxi services or pre-booked rides (e.g., Uber or Bolt are commonly used and considered safe).

No vaccines are required for entry, but some are recommended depending on the areas you'll visit. For example, **malaria prophylaxis is recommended** if you're traveling to northeastern regions like **Kruger National Park or Limpopo Province**, especially during the rainy season. Basic vaccinations like **hepatitis A, typhoid,** and **routine shots (MMR, tetanus)** are also advised.

Consult the U.S. Centers for Disease Control and Prevention (CDC) for travel health advice at **https://wwwnc.cdc.gov/travel/destinations/traveler/none/south-africa**

Customs Entitlements and Monetary Restrictions

Travelers entering South Africa may bring in up to **R25,000** (**approx. $1,300 USD**) in South African Rand without declaring it. Foreign currency is **unrestricted**, but **amounts of $10,000 USD or more** (**or equivalent in other currencies**) must be **declared to customs** on arrival. This includes traveler's cheques and negotiable instruments. Failure to declare large sums can result in **confiscation** and **penalties.**

Travelers **18 years and older** may import the following items **duty-free**, provided they are **for personal use only** and not for resale:

- 200 cigarettes, 20 cigars
- 250g of tobacco
- 2 liters of wine
- 1 liter of spirits or other alcohol
- 50ml perfume and 250ml eau de toilette
- Gifts or souvenirs up to **R5,000** (**approx. $260 USD**) in value

Goods over this threshold are subject to **20% customs duty**, plus **VAT.**

Visitors may bring in **personal electronics** like **laptops, cameras, and phones** for **non-commercial use** without paying duty. If traveling in and out of the country frequently, **registering high-value items** with customs is advisable.[8]

For official customs forms, traveler declarations, and updated rules, visit the **South African Revenue Service** (**SARS**) website at **https://www.sars.gov.za/customs-and-excise/travellers/**.

8 https://www.sars.gov.za/customs-and-excise/travellers/personal-effects-and-household-goods/

Restricted and Prohibited Items[9]

When traveling to South Africa, it's important to be aware of the country's customs laws, which distinguish between prohibited and restricted items. **Prohibited items** are outright banned and may not be brought into the country under any circumstances. **Restricted items** require permits or special clearance before they can legally enter South Africa.

The following items are **not allowed into South Africa** under any conditions:

- Narcotic and habit-forming drugs in any form
- Fully automatic, military and unnumbered weapons
- Explosives and fireworks
- Poison and other toxic substances
- Cigarettes with a mass of more than 2kg per 1 000
- Goods to which a trade description or trademark is applied in contravention of any Act (for example, counterfeit goods)
- Unlawful reproductions of any works subject to copyright
- Penitentiary or prison-made goods

Certain goods **may only be imported if you are in possession of approval from relevant authority.** Such goods on approval will require permit, letter of authority etc. Examples are:

- Firearms / Weapons
- Gold coins
- Excess currency (cash, banknotes etc.)
- Unprocessed minerals (e.g. gold, diamonds, etc.)
- Animals, plants and their products (e.g. animal skins, dairy products, honey)

---

9 https://www.sars.gov.za/customs-and-excise/travellers/arrival-in-sa/

- Medicine (excluding sufficient quantities for three months for own personal treatment accompanied by a letter or certified prescription from a registered physician)
- Herbal products (Department of Health permit required)

South African customs officials have the authority to **inspect, detain, and seize** any item they suspect is in violation of customs law. It is highly recommended that travelers **declare all items of concern** on arrival and check in advance whether permits or approvals are needed. Bringing prohibited or undeclared restricted items into South Africa can result in **serious legal consequences**, including **immediate confiscation** of the item(s), **heavy fines** depending on the nature and value of the item, **detention or arrest**, especially in cases involving drugs, weapons, or counterfeit goods, **prosecution**, which may lead to imprisonment or deportation, and **delays in immigration or customs clearance.**

For a complete and regularly updated list of prohibited and restricted goods, visit the **South African Revenue Service (SARS)** official page at **https://www.sars.gov.za/customs-and-excise/travellers/prohibited-and-restricted-goods/**.

Five Practical Tips to Know Before You Go

1. **Be Mindful of Safety:** South Africa is beautiful but has areas with high crime rates. Stick to well-populated places, avoid walking alone at night, and ask locals or hotel staff for guidance on safe areas.
2. **Rent a Car (and Drive on the Left):** South Africa is vast, and public transportation is limited outside major cities. Renting a car is the best way to explore regions like the Garden Route or Kruger National Park—but remember, they drive on the left!

3. **Tip Generously and Know When to Tip:** Tipping is customary: 10–15% at restaurants, a few dollars for petrol attendants (they pump gas for you), and small tips for parking guards or hotel porters are appreciated.
4. **Use Sun Protection:** South Africa has a hot, sunny climate, especially in summer (November–March). Bring sunscreen, a hat, and sunglasses—even in cooler months.
5. **Have Local Currency (South African Rand):** Card payments are widely accepted in cities, but rural areas, markets, and small vendors often require cash. ATMs are readily available, but always withdraw in safe, well-lit places.

CHAPTER 3

CRIME IN SOUTH AFRICA

IN THIS CHAPTER

- Overview
- Crime Hotspots in South Africa
- Crime Statistics
- Quick Safety Tips

CHAPTER 3

CRIME IN SOUTH AFRICA

Overview

South Africa is generally considered to be **a high-crime country**, with safety **varying significantly by area and context**. While millions of people live and travel in South Africa without incident, the country struggles with one of the highest violent crime rates in the world. Tourists are rarely the targets of serious crime, but **petty theft, muggings, carjackings,** and **robberies** do occur, especially in urban areas like Johannesburg, Cape Town, and Durban. In contrast, rural regions, private game reserves, and well-secured tourist areas are typically safer, especially when travelers remain vigilant and follow local advice. Still, general safety in South Africa remains a concern, particularly for its residents, and public confidence in law enforcement is low. This assessment is supported by the Global Peace Index, which consistently ranks South Africa among the less peaceful countries globally.[10]

Several factors contribute to the high crime rate in South Africa. One of the most significant is **extreme economic inequality**. South Africa has one of the highest Gini coefficients globally, reflecting vast disparities between rich and poor.[11] Alongside this, the **unemployment rate**—over 30% as of 2024—is among the highest in the world, especially among

10 https://www.visionofhumanity.org/maps/#/

11 https://www.worldbank.org/en/country/southafrica/overview

young people.[12] These conditions foster poverty, frustration, and desperation, which in turn fuel various types of criminal activity. **Rapid urbanization** has led to densely populated informal settlements where access to basic services and police protection is limited. In some cities, particularly Cape Town, **organized criminal networks**, including gangs involved in drugs and extortion, have exacerbated violence. Compounding these issues are **under-resourced and overstretched police services**, as well as instances of corruption and inefficiency, which have undermined public trust in law enforcement institutions.[13]

In terms of crime trends over time, South Africa has witnessed a complex and often alarming pattern. According to the South African Police Service (SAPS), the country recorded 27,494 murders in the 2022–2023 reporting period, equating to approximately 45 murders per 100,000 people—one of the highest national murder rates in the world.[14] For comparison, the global average is roughly 6 per 100,000, as noted by the United Nations Office on Drugs and Crime (UNODC).[15] While the COVID-19 lockdowns in 2020 temporarily suppressed crime rates due to movement restrictions and curfews, those gains were short-lived. Since 2021, violent crime—including murder, attempted murder, and gender-based violence—has been rising. The third quarter of 2023 saw a particularly steep increase in murder rates and aggravated robberies, with the Western Cape and Gauteng provinces showing significant spikes.

Property crimes such as **burglary, theft,** and **vehicle hijackings** also remain **widespread**. Although these crimes are frequently underreported, especially in lower-income communities, they contribute heavily to the general perception of insecurity. At the same time, a newer threat is on the rise: cybercrime. As internet use and mobile banking become more common, so too has the prevalence of **digital scams, fraud,** and

12 https://www.statssa.gov.za/?page_id=1856&PPN=P0211

13 https://issafrica.org/crimehub

14 https://www.saps.gov.za/services/crimestats.php

15 https://dataunodc.un.org

identity theft, which have become a growing concern for businesses and individuals alike.[16]

Crime Hotspots in South Africa

Certain areas of South Africa experience particularly high rates of violent and property crime, making them identifiable crime hotspots. While crime occurs throughout the country, **urban centers and surrounding townships tend to report the highest rates**, particularly for violent offenses such as murder, armed robbery, assault, and carjacking.

Cape Town remains one of the most crime-affected cities in the country. While popular tourist areas such as the V&A Waterfront, Table Mountain, and Constantia are generally safe with strong security presence, the broader **Cape Flats region**—including neighborhoods like Mitchells Plain, Manenberg, Nyanga, and Hanover Park—is plagued by **gang-related violence, drug trafficking, and high homicide rates**. In fact, the Nyanga police precinct consistently reports some of the highest murder rates in the country. According to the South African Police Service's 2023 crime statistics, the Western Cape province saw over 4,000 murders in a year, much of it concentrated in these hotspots.[17]

Johannesburg, South Africa's largest city, is another high-crime zone. Suburbs such as **Hillbrow, Yeoville, and Berea** are known for street crime, armed robbery, and violent incidents. Central Business Districts (CBDs) in Johannesburg and Pretoria are also high-risk areas, especially after dark. In contrast, wealthier northern suburbs like Sandton and Rosebank have improved security and lower crime rates but still require caution.

Durban, particularly areas like **KwaMashu, Umlazi, and the CBD**, experiences significant levels of violent crime, including murders and assaults. The province of KwaZulu-Natal also sees high levels of political and factional violence, especially in smaller towns and rural areas. The

16 https://www.saps.gov.za/services/cybercrime.php

17 https://www.saps.gov.za/services/crimestats.php

Eastern Cape, especially towns like **Mthatha and East London**, reports some of the country's highest murder and assault rates per capita. Rural regions here often lack adequate police coverage and are known for high rates of interpersonal violence.

For updated, government-issued safety advice, travelers should consult their country's official travel advisory websites, such as United States Department of State – South Africa Travel Advisory: at **https://travel.state.gov/content/travel/en/traveladvisories/traveladvisories/south-africa-travel-advisory.html.**

As of 2024, South Africa is listed at **Level 2: Exercise Increased Caution** due to crime and civil unrest. However, it's important to note that crime in South Africa is highly localized. Just as there are safe and unsafe areas in major U.S. cities, South Africa also has many low-crime districts, gated communities, and tourist destinations that are patrolled and secure. The key is **vigilance, situational awareness, and adherence to local guidance.**

Crime Statistics

South Africa experiences some of the highest crime rates globally, with **violent crime being especially prevalent.** According to the South African Police Service (SAPS), the country. The most widespread forms of crime in South Africa include **murder, assault, armed robbery, burglary**, and **vehicle-related theft.** In the 2022–2023 period, more than 124,000 cases of assault with intent to inflict grievous bodily harm were reported, and there were over 10,500 reported cases of sexual assault. **Gender-based violence** remains a persistent national crisis, with cases of domestic abuse and rape occurring at alarming levels. **Robbery**, including common robbery and armed house invasions, is another major concern, with nearly 20,000 carjackings recorded in one year alone. **Residential burglaries** are common across all provinces, especially in urban and peri-urban areas. Additionally, **cybercrime** has become a growing threat as more citizens adopt online banking and mobile services.

When compared internationally, South Africa's crime levels stand out starkly. For instance, its murder rate is over six times higher than that of the United States, which recorded around 7 homicides per 100,000 people in 2022, according to the U.S. Centers for Disease Control and Prevention.[18] In Western Europe, homicide rates are typically between 0.5 and 2 per 100,000. Regionally, South Africa's crime rates are significantly higher than those of neighboring countries such as Botswana and Namibia, although differences in crime reporting infrastructure and underreporting make direct comparisons difficult.

The **effectiveness of law enforcement** in South Africa is a source of major concern. The South African Police Service has been widely criticized for being **under-resourced, poorly trained,** and **occasionally corrupt.** Public trust in the police is low, and many citizens believe law enforcement officials are either unable or unwilling to respond to crime appropriately. Corruption, poor case follow-up, slow response times, and a backlog in forensic analysis all contribute to a situation in which criminals frequently act with impunity.[19] The inefficacy of formal law enforcement has led to the growth of a large private security industry, which now employs more personnel than the SAPS itself.

Tourists and foreign visitors are typically not the primary targets of violent crimes, but they are vulnerable to opportunistic and non-violent offenses. Common risks include **pickpocketing, bag-snatching,** and **scams** in crowded or tourist-heavy areas such as public transport hubs and marketplaces. **ATM fraud, credit card skimming,** and **theft from parked vehicles** are also prevalent. Although incidents involving tourists are relatively rare compared to those affecting locals, muggings, armed robbery, and even hotel break-ins have been reported in some cases, especially in less secure neighborhoods or when individuals travel alone at night.

18 https://www.cdc.gov/nchs/hus/contents2019.htm

19 https://issafrica.org/crimehub

Quick Safety Tips

- Avoid walking alone at night, especially in city centers. Keep smartphones, jewelry, and cameras out of sight. Stay in well-trafficked areas and maintain a low profile.
- Stay in hotels or guesthouses with good security (e.g., gated entry, safes, and 24/7 reception), especially in areas like Sandton (Johannesburg) or the V&A Waterfront (Cape Town). Avoid booking in remote or poorly lit areas.
- Avoid hailing unmarked taxis or accepting unsolicited rides. Use apps like Uber or Bolt and confirm the license plate and driver's name before entering. If renting a car, keep windows up and doors locked at all times, especially in traffic.
- Use ATMs inside malls or bank branches during the day. Criminals often target people at standalone machines or after cash withdrawals. Never accept help from strangers at ATMs.
- South Africa is culturally diverse, and understanding basic etiquette can improve safety and interactions. When visiting townships or rural areas, go with a registered local guide. This supports community tourism and helps you avoid unsafe zones.

CHAPTER 4

CRIMINAL LAW VIOLATIONS

IN THIS CHAPTER

- Marijuana and Other Drugs in South Africa
- Prescription Medication
- Penalties
- General Questions
- Law of the Land Hypothetical
- Takeaways

CHAPTER 4

CRIMINAL LAW VIOLATIONS

Marijuana and Other Drugs in South Africa

Cannabis, known locally as "**dagga**," has a long cultural and historical presence in South Africa. It has been used by indigenous groups for centuries, particularly in rural areas like the Eastern Cape and KwaZulu-Natal. These communities traditionally used cannabis for medicinal, spiritual, and recreational purposes. However, colonial-era laws and later apartheid policies criminalized cannabis use, often targeting Black South Africans and disrupting traditional cultivation and use. This long history of racialized enforcement has shaped the country's modern approach to cannabis law, which is increasingly shifting toward decriminalization and regulated personal use.[20]

South Africa distinguishes between medical and recreational cannabis use. **Medicinal cannabis is legal under specific conditions.** Products containing THC (the psychoactive compound in cannabis) are classified as Schedule 6 substances, which means they **can be prescribed only by a medical doctor and dispensed with authorization from the South African Health Products Regulatory Authority** (SAHPRA). **Cannabidiol (CBD), another component of the cannabis plant, is more widely available.** Products that contain less than 20 milligrams of CBD per day and less than 0.001% THC are legal to sell over the counter

20 https://www.africanliberty.org/2021/11/02/south-africas-racist-and-classist-history-of-cannabis-regulation/

without a prescription. These are often used in wellness products like oils, capsules, and skincare treatments.[21]

Recreational cannabis use is decriminalized for private, personal use. In September 2018, the Constitutional Court ruled that adults have the constitutional right to consume and cultivate cannabis for personal use in private settings. This ruling laid the foundation for the **Cannabis for Private Purposes Act**, which was signed into law in **May 2024.** Under this law, adults can legally possess **up to 600 grams of dried cannabis per person in a private space, or 100 grams in a public place, and may cultivate up to four flowering plants per adult.** Despite this, **selling cannabis or using it in public remains illegal.** Any cannabis transported must be secured in such a way that it is not accessible to vehicle occupants.[22]

In terms of commerce, **the legal cannabis industry is restricted.** While there has been increasing interest in establishing a cannabis economy, regulations still limit its commercialization. **The manufacture, import, distribution, and sale of edible cannabis and hemp-based foodstuffs were explicitly banned** in March 2025 by the Minister of Health, creating challenges for businesses hoping to market cannabis edibles or drinks.

Synthetic cannabinoids, often sold under names like **"Spice"** or **"K2,"** are **not directly addressed in South African drug laws,** making enforcement difficult. These substances are often legal by default and are commonly used among youth in urban areas. They can be far more potent than natural THC, posing significant health risks such as psychosis, heart irregularities, and severe agitation. A notable variant is known locally as **"Wiz,"** which has been spreading among school-aged users and has prompted concern from public health officials and law enforcement.

Beyond cannabis, South Africa has **stringent drug laws for other substances.** The Drugs and Drug Trafficking Act 140 of 1992 classifies

21 https://leafwell.com/blog/is-marijuana-legal-in-south-africa?

22 https://www.gov.za/documents/acts/cannabis-private-purposes-act-7-2024-english-sepedi-03-jun-2024?

substances such as heroin, cocaine, methamphetamine (locally known as "tik"), Ecstasy, and Mandrax as **prohibited. Possession** of these substances can lead to prison sentences of **up to 15 years**, while **trafficking or dealing** may result in **up to 25 years** in prison. The law is enforced strictly, and penalties are severe even for relatively small quantities. A significant public health issue in South Africa is **"nyaope"** (also known as **whoonga**), a dangerous street drug that combines heroin, cannabis, and crushed antiretroviral medication. Nyaope is prevalent in townships and has been linked to high addiction rates among youth.

Although cannabis is now more legally accepted in South Africa, **the broader drug policy remains prohibitive and punitive in nature**. There are ongoing calls from activists and civil society for drug law reform to focus more on harm reduction and health-based approaches. South Africa's economic interest in cannabis is growing, particularly as the global cannabis market continues to expand. As of 2025, the legal cannabis market in South Africa remains underdeveloped due to regulatory limitations, but investment continues to flow into the sector, with projections that the industry could be worth over 100 billion South African Rand (about $5.3 billion USD) by the early 2030s if fully legalized and commercialized.[23]

Prescription Medication

When traveling to South Africa with prescription or over the counter (OTC) medications, there are important regulations and limitations travelers must observe to avoid legal complications. The South African Health Products Regulatory Authority (SAHPRA), along with customs authorities, enforces strict controls to prevent misuse and illegal distribution of pharmaceutical substances.

Travelers are allowed to bring prescription medications into South Africa for **personal use**, but this is subject to certain conditions. You may carry up to a **30-day supply** of prescribed medication, provided that you have

23 https://www.aljazeera.com/news/2024/6/10/south-africa-legalises-cannabis-use-will-the-rest-of-africa-follow

a valid prescription issued by a licensed medical practitioner. The medication must be **in its original packaging**, properly labeled with your name, dosage instructions, and prescribing doctor's information. It is strongly recommended to carry a letter from your doctor stating your medical condition and the necessity of the medication, especially if the drug falls under **controlled substances** such as opioids, stimulants (e.g., ADHD medication like Adderall), or sedatives.

If the medication you're bringing contains a **scheduled substance**—such as Schedule 5 or 6 drugs under South African law—you may require **pre-approval** or a special permit from SAHPRA. Common examples include strong painkillers, sleeping pills, anti-anxiety drugs, or medications that contain narcotic ingredients. Bringing these into the country without proper documentation or permits can result in **confiscation, fines**, or even **arrest**, particularly if quantities suggest intent to distribute rather than personal use.

Over-the-counter medications are also subject to regulation, though less strictly. Many common OTC drugs, such as antihistamines, ibuprofen, or cold medications, are permitted in reasonable quantities for personal use.

However, some OTC products available in other countries may contain ingredients classified as **prescription-only or restricted** in South Africa. For example, pseudoephedrine—a common decongestant—has usage limits due to its potential for abuse in manufacturing illegal substances. Carrying large quantities without documentation can raise red flags with customs.

Failure to comply with South Africa's medication import laws can lead to a **range of penalties**, including the **confiscation of the medicine**, **fines**, **entry denial**, or even **criminal charges** if controlled substances are involved. To avoid such issues, travelers are advised to check with the South African embassy or consulate in their home country and consult SAHPRA or the South African Revenue Service (SARS) before traveling.

Penalties

South Africa's legal penalties for drug offenses are determined by the **Drugs and Drug Trafficking Act 140 of 1992** and the **Cannabis for Private Purposes Act 7 of 2024**, as well as court precedent, particularly the 2018 *Prince* judgment. The severity of penalties depends on the type of substance, quantity involved, location of the offense (public vs. private), and whether the offense involves possession, trafficking, or production.

Penalties for drug offenses in South Africa include **up to 2 years in prison** for **cannabis possession that exceeds legal limits. Selling or distributing cannabis** can lead to a prison sentence of **up to 15 years. Using or possessing cannabis in public,** even within legal quantity limits, may result in **up to 2 years in prison. Cultivating cannabis** beyond the legally allowed number of plants can also lead to a prison sentence of **up to 15 years. Possession or sale of synthetic cannabinoids** carries a penalty of **up to 15 years in prison. For harder drugs** like heroin, cocaine, methamphetamine, LSD, or ecstasy, possession can result in **up to 15 years in prison**, while **trafficking or manufacturing** can lead to a sentence of **up to 25 years.**

General Questions

1. ***Is cannabis legal in South Africa?* Yes.** Cannabis is **legal for personal use by adults in private settings** in South Africa. This includes possession, consumption, and cultivation at home within specific limits. However, **public use, distribution, and commercial sale remain illegal.**

2. ***Where can I legally purchase marijuana in South Africa?*** You **cannot legally purchase marijuana** in South Africa at a store or dispensary. The **sale of cannabis is still illegal**, including gifting it to someone else. The law only allows for private cultivation and personal use, meaning adults must **grow their own.**

3. ***Can I have marijuana on my person or in hotel room in South Africa?* Yes.** You can legally have marijuana on your person or in a hotel room in South Africa, but only within the legal possession limits: **up to 100 grams in public** (such as on your person while walking or traveling) and **up to 600 grams in private**, such as in your hotel room. However, **you cannot use or display cannabis in public**, and hotels may have their own policies prohibiting possession or use on their property, even if it's technically legal.

4. ***Are there any other exceptions to the possession and consumption of cannabis in South Africa?* Yes.** There are exceptions to possession and consumption. **Minors** (**under 18**) are not permitted to possess or use cannabis under any circumstances. It is also illegal to use cannabis **in** front of children, near schools, or in any way that exposes minors to cannabis. **Driving under the influence of cannabis** is a criminal offense. Additionally, while adults may grow their own cannabis for private use, **sharing, gifting, or selling it is illegal.** Any cannabis use or cultivation that creates a public nuisance or endangers others may also be prosecuted.

5. ***What are the penalties for possessing and consuming other types of illicit drugs in South Africa?*** Possessing or consuming illicit drugs (e.g., heroin, cocaine, meth, LSD, ecstasy) in South Africa is a serious offense. **Possession** can result in up to **15 years in prison,** even for small amounts. **Trafficking, manufacturing, or distributing** these drugs can lead to up to **25 years in prison** and large fines. The law is strictly enforced, and there are **no exceptions** for tourists or foreign nationals.

Law of the Land Hypothetical

HYPOTHETICAL: *John, a tourist from the United States, visits South Africa for a vacation. He brings a small quantity of marijuana (about 50 grams) for personal use, thinking it would be fine since he's aware that cannabis is legalized for personal use in private settings. While at a hotel in Cape Town, he consumes some cannabis in his hotel room, but the hotel staff reports the smell to local authorities. Is John legally allowed to possess and consume marijuana in his hotel room, and what penalties might he face for his actions?*

ANSWER: *John can legally possess up to 600 grams of cannabis in a private space like his hotel room. However,* ***consumption in public*** *or in a way noticeable to others (such as hotel staff) is illegal. Since staff reported the smell, John may face a penalty for* ***public consumption****, which could lead to* ***a fine or up to 2 years in prison****. If he had kept consumption discreet, he would have avoided legal issues. The hotel's policies and staff complaints complicate the case, highlighting the importance of respecting public consumption laws.*

Takeaways

- Adults can legally possess and consume cannabis in private settings (up to 600g of dried cannabis), but public use remains illegal and can lead to penalties.
- Consuming cannabis in public spaces is punishable by up to 2 years in prison.
- Selling, distributing, or gifting cannabis (even without profit) remains illegal, with severe penalties of up to 15 years in prison.
- Possessing or trafficking other illicit drugs (like heroin, cocaine, or meth) can result in up to 15 years in prison for possession and up to 25 years for trafficking.
- While personal use is allowed, there is no legal way to purchase cannabis in South Africa from stores or dispensaries.

CHAPTER 5

ALCOHOL-RELATED OFFENSES

IN THIS CHAPTER

- Alcohol-Related Offenses
- Alcohol Regulation
- Things to Remember
- General Questions
- Law of the Land Hypothetical
- Takeaways

CHAPTER 5

ALCOHOL-RELATED OFFENSES

Alcohol-Related Offenses

Alcohol has a deep cultural and historical presence in South Africa. Historically, alcohol consumption was introduced during the colonial era by European settlers, which shaped the drinking culture in the country. Traditional alcoholic beverages were consumed by indigenous groups, and over time, stronger European drinks like beer, wine, and spirits became more common. In modern South Africa, alcohol is associated with socializing, celebrations, and rituals, but it also plays a role in social challenges like alcohol abuse.

In everyday life, alcohol is widely consumed during social events, family gatherings, and holidays such as Freedom Day and the Day of Reconciliation. Beer and wine are especially popular, with a strong presence in bars, restaurants, and homes. South Africa has a robust wine industry, especially in the **Western Cape**, and alcoholic drinks like **beer, wine, brandy, and cider** are commonly enjoyed by locals and tourists alike. Alcohol is particularly associated with socializing and is often shared among friends and family in communal settings.

Alcohol is **legal** and easily accessible in South Africa, available for purchase in liquor stores, bars, restaurants, and supermarkets. The **legal drinking age** is **18 years**, and alcohol is available from **9 AM to 6 PM** during weekdays, with extended hours on weekends. However, there are restrictions on drinking in public spaces, and driving under the influence is illegal. South Africa has strict laws surrounding alcohol-related offenses.

Alcohol Regulation

In South Africa, alcohol consumption is governed by several regulations aimed at controlling its availability and use. One of the key regulations is the **Liquor Act of 2003**, which outlines the legal framework for the production, distribution, and consumption of alcohol. This act establishes the legal drinking age, the hours during which alcohol can be sold, and guidelines for the licensing of alcohol outlets. The act also governs the prohibition of drinking in public places and the regulations regarding drunk driving.

There are **restrictions on alcohol advertising** in South Africa. The advertising of alcoholic beverages is regulated by the **Advertising Standards Authority of South Africa** (**ASA**), which ensures that advertisements do not target minors, promote irresponsible drinking, or encourage dangerous behavior such as drinking and driving. Additionally, advertisements must not mislead the public regarding the effects of alcohol or promote excessive consumption. Alcohol advertising is prohibited during programs primarily aimed at children, and there are strict rules around the content and timing of alcohol-related ads on television, radio, and in print media.

Enforcement of alcohol regulations is carried out by law enforcement agencies such as the **South African Police Service** (**SAPS**), local municipalities, and the **Liquor Board**. Police are responsible for checking the legal age of alcohol consumers and ensuring that laws on public drinking and drunk driving are followed. Alcohol outlets are regularly inspected to ensure they comply with licensing laws, and there are penalties for operating without a license or selling alcohol to underage customers. The government also conducts random alcohol checks, especially during holidays or public events. Violations of alcohol-related laws can result in **fines, imprisonment, or the revocation of licenses** for businesses that fail to comply with the regulations.

Things to Remember

- **Drinking Age:** The legal drinking age in South Africa is **18 years old**. Anyone under the age of 18 is prohibited from purchasing or consuming alcohol.
- **ID:** You are required to show **valid identification** when purchasing alcohol to verify that you are at least 18 years old. Alcohol outlets, including stores and bars, are legally obligated to check the age of customers before selling alcohol.
- **Public Consumption:** It is generally **illegal** to consume alcohol in public places such as streets, parks, and beaches, unless specifically authorized. Carrying open alcohol containers in public is also prohibited in many areas. Some local municipalities may have specific by-laws allowing alcohol consumption in designated public spaces (local regulations may vary).
- **Public Drunkenness:** Public drunkenness, or being visibly intoxicated in public spaces, can result in a fine or arrest. While there isn't a fixed national penalty for public drunkenness, individuals may face **fines**, **detention**, or other local sanctions, depending on the situation and local enforcement.
- **Drunk Driving:** Legal **blood alcohol limit** for drivers in South Africa is **0.05%** for private drivers and **0.02%** for commercial drivers (e.g., bus and taxi drivers). Penalties for driving under the influence include **fines**, **license suspension**, and in some cases, **imprisonment**. Serious offenses may result in up to **6 years in prison**, depending on the severity of the case.
- **Purchase of Alcohol:** Alcohol can be legally purchased in **liquor stores, bars, restaurants**, and **supermarkets**. However, sales are restricted by hours. Generally, alcohol can be sold from **9 AM to 6 PM** on weekdays, with extended hours on weekends. In some provinces, restrictions may vary, and there are **dry areas** or **licensed venues** where alcohol sales are prohibited.
- **Alcohol Permits:** If you're hosting a public or private event with alcohol in South Africa, you may be required to obtain an **alcohol license or permit**. The requirements depend on the size and

nature of the event. **Temporary event permits** are often needed for larger gatherings, festivals, or parties where alcohol is served to the public. Local municipalities are responsible for issuing these permits.

- **Illegal Alcohol:** Illegal alcohol, also known as **"moonshine"**, is an issue in South Africa, particularly in rural areas. It poses significant health risks due to unregulated production methods. Concerns about **unsafe alcohol, counterfeit alcohol**, and **alcohol poisoning** have led to public health campaigns against illegal alcohol production. Authorities have cracked down on illegal alcohol, but it remains a persistent problem in certain areas.

General Questions

1. ***Can I possess an open container in public?*** **No.** Possessing an open container of alcohol in public is generally **not allowed** in South Africa. Drinking alcohol or carrying open containers in public spaces such as streets, parks, or beaches is typically **prohibited by municipal by-laws.** Violations can result in **fines or arrest**, depending on the local authority's enforcement policies.

2. ***Is it legal to drink alcohol on beaches or at outdoor festivals in South Africa?*** Drinking alcohol on beaches or at outdoor festivals in South Africa is generally **not allowed**, unless the event has been officially licensed to permit alcohol consumption. Most **public beaches, parks**, and **outdoor venues** fall under municipal by-laws that **prohibit alcohol possession and consumption**, even in open-air settings. Always check local regulations or event permits before consuming alcohol in public.

Law of the Land Hypothetical

HYPOTHETICAL: *Tom, a tourist from the UK, plans to host a birthday party at his Airbnb rental in Durban and wants to serve alcohol to his guests. He wonders if he needs a special permit or if he can serve alcohol freely.*

ANSWER: *No permit is required to serve alcohol at a* **private, non-commercial party** *held in a private residence like an Airbnb, as long as alcohol is* **not being sold**. *However, Tom must still follow noise regulations and avoid public disturbances, as neighbors could file complaints. If Tom were charging guests for alcohol or hosting a public event, a* **temporary liquor license** *would be required under South African liquor law.*

Takeaways

- The legal drinking age is 18, and ID is required to purchase alcohol.
- Public consumption of alcohol—such as drinking on streets, beaches, or parks—is generally prohibited and may lead to fines or arrest.
- Drunk driving laws are strict, with a legal blood alcohol limit of 0.05% for regular drivers and 0.02% for professional drivers, and violations can result in imprisonment or heavy fines.
- Alcohol sales are regulated by time and place, and licenses are required for selling or serving alcohol at public events.
- Bringing your own alcohol to events or outdoor venues is often restricted, and illegal alcohol remains a health and safety concern in some areas.

CHAPTER 6

FIREARM & AMMUNITION OFFENSES

IN THIS CHAPTER

- Current Firearm Status
- Legal Requirements for Purchasing, Carrying, and Using a Firearm
- Firearm Restrictions for Visitors
- Penalties
- General Questions
- Law of the Land True Story
- Takeaways

CHAPTER 6

FIREARM & AMMUNITION OFFENSES

Current Firearm Status[24]

In South Africa, firearm ownership is governed by the **Firearms Control Act of 2000**, which outlines strict eligibility and licensing requirements. To legally own a firearm, a person must:

- Be **at least 21 years old** (some exceptions may apply for sporting or professional use).
- Be a **permanent resident or South African citizen.**
- Pass a **background check** (no history of mental illness, domestic violence, or substance abuse).
- Complete **competency training** and receive a **competency certificate** from the South African Police Service (SAPS).
- Apply for a **firearm license**, which is specific to the type of firearm and intended use (e.g., self-defense, sport shooting, hunting).

South African law distinguishes between different license categories with corresponding possession limits:

24 https://en.wikipedia.org/wiki/Firearms_regulation_in_South_Africa

- **Self-defense:** Typically limited to **one handgun or non-automatic shotgun.**
- **Occasional hunting/sport shooting:** Up to **four firearms** with proper justification.
- **Dedicated hunters/sport shooters (members of accredited associations):** May possess **more than four**, depending on endorsement.
- **Professional use (e.g., security, business):** Requires a business license and is more strictly regulated.

Fully automatic firearms are **prohibited**, while semi-automatics may require special justification and are tightly regulated. Ammunition limits also apply depending on the license type.

Legal Requirements for Purchasing, Carrying, and Using a Firearm

To legally purchase a firearm in South Africa, a person must be **at least 21 years old**, although exceptions can be made under special circumstances. The individual must be **a South African citizen or permanent resident**, **mentally sound**, and **free from substance dependency**. A **clean criminal record** is required, particularly with no history of violent or firearm-related offenses or domestic abuse.[25]

Before purchasing a firearm, the person must undergo accredited **firearm training** and pass a competency assessment. This includes a background check, interviews by the police, and a verification of secure firearm storage at home. Once the individual receives a competency certificate, they may apply for a **firearm license** from the South African Police Service. A valid reason must be given for the firearm (such as self-defense, hunting, or sport shooting), and each firearm requires its own license. Applications must be submitted through a local police station's Designated Firearms Officer and may take several months to

25 https://en.wikipedia.org/wiki/Firearms_regulation_in_South_Africa

process. Once issued, a firearm license is valid for **five to ten years**, depending on the type.[26]

Only the licensed owner is legally allowed to carry a firearm in public. The firearm must be **concealed**, typically in a holster or similar holder, and should never be openly displayed. The owner must carry the license at all times when in possession of the firearm

There are specific areas where carrying a firearm is **prohibited**, such as government buildings, schools, bars, and nightclubs. Private properties may also forbid firearms by posting signs. Entering such spaces with a firearm, even if licensed, is illegal unless express permission is granted or there is a valid legal exemption.

The use of a firearm in South Africa is strictly regulated and permitted only under certain conditions. **It may be used in self-defense when there is an immediate and unlawful threat to life,** but the response must be proportional to the threat faced. The use of lethal force is allowed only when it is the only reasonable option to prevent harm. Firing warning shots or using a firearm to protect property alone is discouraged and may be considered unlawful. **All discharges of a firearm, even in self-defense, must be reported to the South African Police Service.** Misuse of a firearm can result in criminal charges, including murder, attempted murder, or negligent discharge, and the responsibility to prove the action was justified lies with the firearm owner.

Firearm Restrictions for Visitors

South Africa imposes strict firearm regulations on non-citizens and visitors. **Under the Firearms Control Act 60 of 2000, a visitor may not possess, carry, or use a firearm unless they obtain special authorization in the form of a Temporary Import Permit.** This permit is issued only for specific and limited purposes, such as participation in sporting events, film productions, hunting expeditions, or in certain diplomatic

26 https://www.gov.za/documents/firearms-control-act

or official security circumstances. The process is managed by the South African Police Service (SAPS) through the Central Firearms Registry.

To obtain a **Temporary Import Permit**, the visitor must apply in advance, typically with the assistance of a licensed South African firearm dealer, tour outfitter, or event organizer. For example, professional hunters and competitive shooters often rely on South African outfitters to assist with the logistics and legal process of bringing in firearms for short-term use. In cases involving diplomatic or state security personnel, temporary firearm authorizations are handled through intergovernmental arrangements.

The applicant must provide a valid passport, official proof of firearm ownership and licensing from their home country, documentation supporting the purpose of the firearm's use in South Africa—such as an event invitation or hunting permit—and any required export documentation from their country of origin. If the application is approved, the permit allows the visitor to bring in the firearm and use it solely for the authorized activity and within the designated areas and time frames. **Use for general self-defense or recreational purposes outside the approved context is prohibited.**

Visitors are not permitted to purchase firearms in South Africa or permanently possess one while in the country. They may not carry a firearm for personal protection, nor may they rent or borrow a firearm without a valid permit. Any firearm brought into the country must be declared at a designated port of entry, such as an international airport, where SAPS officials will inspect the documentation. Firearms must be stored securely in approved safes and transported in locked containers when not in active use.

Unauthorized possession, misuse, or deviation from the permitted purpose can lead to **serious legal consequences**. These may include confiscation of the firearm, criminal prosecution, fines, imprisonment, and even future travel restrictions or bans from entering South Africa.

WARNING

Penalties[27]

In South Africa, penalties for firearm-related offenses are severe and governed primarily by the **Firearms Control Act 60 of 2000** and the **Criminal Law Amendment Act 105 of 1997. Possession of a firearm** without a valid license is a **criminal offense.** If the firearm is a standard weapon, unlawful possession can lead to **imprisonment**, with the exact duration depending on the circumstances. The Criminal Law Amendment Act mandates a **minimum sentence of 15 years' imprisonment** for the unlawful possession of both automatic and semi-automatic firearms. Courts increasingly impose minimum sentences ranging from 7 to 10 years for standalone offenses involving unlawful possession of semi-automatic firearms, with significantly harsher sentences when such possession is tied to serious crimes like murder or robbery. Offenders may face heavy fines and imprisonment ranging from several years to multiple decades for possessing illegal firearms.

It is also a criminal offense to possess firearms that have been **modified** to discharge multiple shots per trigger pull, changed in caliber or barrel length, or with serial numbers erased or altered without written authorization from the Registrar. Prohibited firearms include fully automatic weapons, rocket or grenade launchers, and similar devices. The possession of these altered or prohibited firearms subjects individuals to severe fines and lengthy prison terms.

Firearm owners are legally required to report the loss or theft of any firearm within 24 hours. Failing to do so is a criminal offense. While prosecutions for negligent loss are not common, the law imposes strict obligations on firearm owners in such situations.

Carrying firearms in designated **firearm-free zones**, such as schools and government buildings, is strictly prohibited and punishable by imprisonment ranging between **five and 25 years.** These zones are

27 https://www.scielo.org.za/scielo.php?pid=S1727-37812020000100008&script=sci

legally enforceable, and the police are empowered to search individuals and seize firearms and ammunition within these areas.

Other firearm-related offenses include discharging a weapon recklessly, using one while under the influence of alcohol or drugs, or handling it in a way that causes injury or property damage. These actions carry varying criminal penalties depending on the severity of the conduct. Additionally, illegal trading, manufacturing, importing, or exporting firearms without proper licenses or permits constitutes a serious criminal offense, punishable by significant prison sentences.[28]

For juveniles, the law distinguishes between different age groups. Children under 12 cannot be prosecuted. Juveniles aged 12 to 17 fall under the Child Justice Act, which emphasizes rehabilitation over punishment. Sentences for these offenders often include community service, correctional supervision, or participation in educational programs. Imprisonment is considered a last resort and is limited in both scope and duration.[29]

General Questions

1. ***What happens if the police catch me carrying a firearm in South Africa?*** In South Africa, carrying a firearm without a valid license is a serious offense under the Firearms Control Act of 2000. If caught, you could face up to 15 years in prison, depending on the circumstances. The firearm will be confiscated, and you may be barred from owning firearms in the future.

28 https://lawfulliving.co.za/book/text/law-enforcement--firearms.html

29 https://www.government.nl/topics/sentences-and-non-punitive-orders/penalties-juvenile-offenders

2. ***What are the penalties for failing to declare a firearm at the airport when entering South Africa?*** Failing to declare a firearm when entering South Africa is a criminal offense. If you arrive at the airport with a firearm and do not report it to the South African Police Service, the firearm will be confiscated, and you could be arrested. This may lead to prosecution for unlawful possession of a firearm, which carries a possible prison sentence of up to 15 years. You could also be fined, deported, or banned from re-entering the country. All firearms must be declared immediately upon arrival, and a Temporary Import Permit must be issued before you can legally possess the weapon in South Africa.

Law of the Land True Story[30]

The tragic shooting of Reeva Steenkamp by Oscar Pistorius in 2013, while widely discussed in the context of femicide, also highlights significant concerns about gun ownership and its implications in South Africa. Pistorius, a former Paralympic athlete, shot and killed his girlfriend after mistaking her for an intruder. This incident underscores the risks of widespread firearm ownership in a country with high levels of violent crime.

South Africa's firearm laws allow for licensed gun ownership, but as evidenced by Pistorius' case, even licensed owners can misuse firearms in domestic settings, leading to devastating consequences. Pistorius' access to a firearm, which he claimed was for self-defense, ultimately escalated a situation that resulted in the loss of life. This tragedy raises critical questions about the effectiveness of firearms for personal safety in a country already struggling with violent crime.

The case has drawn attention to the potential dangers of gun ownership, especially when it involves individuals who may not always use firearms responsibly. Despite strict regulations for obtaining a firearm license in South Africa, such as mandatory background checks and

30 https://www.bbc.com/news/world-africa-67873941

competency tests, incidents like the Pistorius shooting suggest that legal access to firearms does not guarantee safety and can, in some cases, lead to tragic outcomes.

Pistorius' parole, granted after serving half of his sentence, also reignites the debate about how firearms are used in society and this case serves as a stark reminder of how firearms, even when legally acquired, can contribute to unintended violence, especially in high-stress or emotionally charged environments.

Takeaways

- South Africa's Firearms Control Act of 2000 requires individuals to meet several criteria to own a firearm, including being at least 21, passing a background check, completing firearm training, and obtaining a specific license for each firearm based on its intended use.
- Firearm owners must carry their weapons concealed and secure, with certain areas like schools and government buildings being firearm-free zones. Violations can lead to imprisonment.
- Possessing firearms unlawfully, including automatic or semi-automatic weapons, can lead to severe penalties, including a minimum 15-year prison sentence. Failing to report a lost or stolen firearm within 24 hours is also a criminal offense.
- Visitors to South Africa must obtain a Temporary Import Permit to bring in and use firearms for specific purposes like hunting or sports. Unauthorized possession or misuse can lead to prosecution and confiscation.
- Juveniles aged 12-17 who commit firearm offenses are handled under the Child Justice Act, focusing on rehabilitation through community service, correctional supervision, or educational programs rather than imprisonment.

CHAPTER 7

PROSTITUTION

IN THIS CHAPTER

- Overview
- Laws and Penalties
- Prostitution Practices
- Sex Trafficking and Exploitation
- Sex Tourism and Public Health Concerns
- Tips to Avoid Being Solicited
- Law of the Land True Story
- Takeaways

CHAPTER 7
PROSTITUTION

Overview

Prostitution in South Africa is **currently illegal** for both the buying and selling of sex, as well as related activities such as brothel keeping and pimping. This means that both the sex workers and their clients can be prosecuted under the law. South Africa's government has been under pressure from advocacy groups to decriminalize sex work to protect workers' rights, but this has yet to happen.

The socio-economic factors that drive prostitution in South Africa are deeply rooted in **poverty, inequality**, and **unemployment**. The country's high levels of economic inequality, especially among women, contribute to a situation where individuals, particularly those from marginalized communities, may turn to sex work as a means of survival. Limited education, lack of access to healthcare, and the need to support families often force women and, to a lesser extent, men into the sex trade.

In addition, the high rates of **gender-based violence** and the vulnerability of women in South Africa further exacerbate the situation, with many being coerced into the sex trade through circumstances of abuse or trafficking. Economic hardship, coupled with the lack of social safety nets, contributes to individuals entering prostitution either as a last resort or due to systemic pressures.

Societal attitudes toward prostitution in South Africa are largely negative, often **stigmatizing sex workers and viewing them as criminals or victims**. This stigma is reinforced by traditional values, religious teachings, and cultural beliefs about sexuality. Many South Africans view prostitution as immoral, and sex workers are frequently marginalized or treated as disposable. Nevertheless, there is a growing movement of support for the decriminalization of sex work, particularly from human rights groups and some political voices, who argue that decriminalization would lead to better protection for sex workers, reducing violence, and increasing access to health services.

Laws and Penalties

Prostitution is prohibited under the **Criminal Law (Sexual Offences and Related Matters) Amendment Act, 2007**, which criminalizes engaging in sexual acts for reward, effectively making both sex workers and their clients liable to prosecution. The South African Law Reform Commission has explored potential reforms, including decriminalization, but as of now, no legislative changes have been enacted.[31]

There are **no designated legal zones** for prostitution in South Africa. Sex workers often operate in public spaces, which exposes them to legal risks and harassment. Municipal by-laws may include provisions related to prostitution, but these are typically aimed at regulating public order rather than providing legal protection for sex work.

Under the current legal framework, there are **no official requirements or protections** for sex workers. This lack of legal recognition leaves sex workers vulnerable to exploitation, violence, and discrimination. Advocacy groups like the **Asijiki Coalition** and **Sex Workers Education and Advocacy Task Force (SWEAT)** have been actively campaigning for the decriminalization of sex work to ensure the rights and safety of sex workers.

31 https://en.wikipedia.org/wiki/Prostitution_in_South_Africa

Prostitution is punishable by law with the following offenses and penalties:

- Engaging in unlawful carnal intercourse for reward (selling or buying sex) is a criminal offense.
- Keeping or managing a brothel, or aiding in its operation, is a crime, with penalties applying to owners, tenants, and managers aware of the brothel's use.
- Procuring, pimping, and living off the earnings of prostitution are criminalized with penalties.
- Solicitation in public, refusing to provide identification when requested by police in a brothel, or being found in a brothel without disclosure of the keeper's identity are also offenses.
- The law criminalizes acts of indecency for reward, such as sexual acts or indecent exposure.

Penalties may include fines, imprisonment, or both and can apply to both sex workers and their clients. Enforcement is reported to be inconsistent, and sex workers frequently face arrest, harassment, and violence, including from law enforcement officials, deterring them from seeking legal recourse or reporting crimes.

Prostitution Practices

Estimates suggest that there are between 131,000 and 182,000 sex workers in South Africa, which accounts for approximately 0.76% to 1% of the adult population. Among these, most are female sex workers, with a reported average age of debut around 24 years and average duration in the industry spanning 12 years. Many sex workers support multiple dependents, illustrating the economic role sex work plays for individuals and families. The **HIV prevalence** among sex workers is high, with **national rates near 60%** and variation across cities, such as 71.8% in Johannesburg and 39.7% in Cape Town.[32]

32 https://www.developmentaid.org/news-stream/post/156843/sex-workers-in-south-africa

Sex work in South Africa takes various forms. **Street-based sex work** is the most visible and involves individuals soliciting clients in public spaces. This form is often associated with higher risks of violence and police harassment. **Brothel-based sex work** occurs in establishments such as massage parlors or private homes. A study in Cape Town identified 103 brothels, with 67 operating from residential houses and 34 as clubs or massage parlors. **Escort services**, where sex workers operate independently or through agencies, are also common, often using online platforms for advertising. The rise of **online sex work**, including webcam modeling and phone sex, has become more prevalent, especially during the COVID-19 pandemic. However, this shift has also introduced new risks, such as cyber abuse and exploitation.

Local authorities' attitudes toward prostitution are mixed. While the practice is illegal, enforcement is inconsistent, with law enforcement sometimes conducting raids and making arrests. However, there are **significant concerns about police abuse**, with many sex workers reporting violence and harassment from officers. Advocacy groups like the **Asijiki Coalition** and **SWEAT (Sex Workers Education and Advocacy Task Force)** are campaigning for the decriminalization of sex work, arguing that it would reduce violence, improve access to healthcare, and better protect the rights of sex workers. In December 2022, the South African government announced plans to decriminalize sex work in an effort to diminish crime and safeguard the well-being of sex workers.

Sex Trafficking and Exploitation

Sex trafficking and exploitation are significant concerns in South Africa, driven by factors such as poverty, unemployment, and social inequality. These conditions create vulnerabilities that traffickers exploit, leading to both domestic and transnational trafficking activities.

South Africa serves as a source, transit, and destination country for trafficking. Traffickers exploit individuals' vulnerabilities, often luring them with false promises of employment or better living conditions. The demand for cheap labor and commercial sex, combined with weak law enforcement and corruption, exacerbates the problem. Especially urban centers like **Johannesburg, Cape Town, Durban**, and **Bloemfontein** are **hotspots for trafficking** due to their economic activities and transportation networks. These cities attract both internal and cross-border trafficking, with victims often ending up in informal settlements where oversight is minimal.

Women and children are the most affected by sex trafficking in South Africa. Girls are often trafficked for commercial sexual exploitation and domestic servitude, while boys may be forced into labor-intensive roles. Migrant populations, including those from neighboring countries like Zimbabwe and Mozambique, are particularly vulnerable due to their precarious legal status and lack of support networks.

The South African government has taken steps to combat trafficking, including the enactment of the **Prevention and Combating of Trafficking in Persons Act in 2013.** This legislation provides a legal framework for addressing trafficking offenses and protecting victims. Additionally, the government has developed a National Policy Framework to guide the implementation of anti-trafficking measures. However, challenges remain in enforcement, victim identification, and prosecution of offenders.

Sex Tourism and Public Health

Sex tourism is present in South Africa, particularly in major urban centers which attract both domestic and international tourists, with the demand for commercial sex services influenced by factors like economic disparities and the country's well-developed tourism infrastructure. While sex tourism is not officially promoted, the prevalence of sex work in these areas contributes to its occurrence.

Sex tourism in South Africa is **not formally organized or advertised** through official channels due to the illegality of prostitution. However, it operates through **informal networks**, including **online platforms, social media, and word-of-mouth.** The anonymity provided by the internet facilitates the arrangement of such services, making regulation and monitoring challenging.

The presence of sex tourism raises **significant public health concerns**, particularly regarding the **spread of HIV/AIDS** and other sexually transmitted infections (STIs). **South Africa has one of the highest HIV prevalence rates globally, with estimates suggesting that approximately 60% of sex workers are HIV positive.** The criminalization of sex work exacerbates these issues by limiting access to healthcare services, promoting unsafe working conditions, and increasing the risk of violence against sex workers. Stigma and discrimination further hinder efforts to provide necessary health interventions and support.

HELPFUL TIPS

Tips to Avoid Being Solicited

- **Avoid known hotspots:** Sex work is more visible in certain urban areas such as parts of Johannesburg (Hillbrow), Cape Town (Long Street, Green Point), and Durban (Point Road). Staying away from these neighborhoods at night or during peak activity times reduces the likelihood of solicitation.
- **Dress and behave conservatively:** Sex workers may be more likely to approach individuals who appear to be tourists, wealthy, or alone. Dressing modestly and avoiding behavior that might suggest you're looking for company (e.g., lingering in red-light areas or engaging with street-level solicitors) can help.
- **Choose reputable accommodations:** Stay in well-established hotels that have clear policies against solicitation. High-end hotels often monitor entrances and discourage unauthorized individuals from entering.
- **Limit alcohol intake in nightlife districts:** Bars and clubs in nightlife-heavy areas may be frequented by sex workers. Staying alert and in control, especially in unfamiliar settings, reduces the chance of being approached or misreading a situation.

- **Ignore solicitations:** If approached, do not engage. A polite but firm "No, thank you" followed by walking away is generally effective. Avoid eye contact and prolonged conversation, which may be interpreted as interest.
- **Travel in groups:** Individuals who are alone are more likely to be targeted. Moving in pairs or groups, particularly at night, tends to deter solicitation.

TRUE STORY Law of the Land Hypothetical [33]

In a powerful piece published by *The Conversation*, Dr. Susann Huschke, a postdoctoral researcher in anthropology at the University of the Witwatersrand, amplifies the voice of Zenande Dlamini—a sex worker and activist—who openly criticizes South Africa's National Strategic Plan on HIV, TB, and STIs. While the government's five-year plan aims to tackle the country's persistently high infection rates and includes vulnerable populations like sex workers, Dlamini argues that its promises are largely hollow without structural change, especially the **decriminalization of sex work.**

According to Dlamini, more than half of South Africa's female sex workers in major cities are HIV positive, yet less than a third receive antiretroviral treatment. The government's 90:90:90 goal (diagnosis, treatment, and viral suppression) is, in her view, unrealistic given the lack of resources, trained peer educators, and dedicated organizations—particularly in rural or underserved areas like the Eastern Cape.

She also highlights deeper systemic issues: the criminalization of sex work fuels **police abuse**, **condom confiscation**, **healthcare stigma**, and **barriers to exiting the industry**. Her letter passionately argues that until sex work is decriminalized and real support—like education

33 https://theconversation.com/a-sex-workers-view-on-south-africas-latest-plans-to-beat-hiv-79355

opportunities, drug rehabilitation, and human rights protections—is provided, public health goals will remain out of reach.

Takeaways

- Prostitution is criminalized in South Africa. Both the act of selling and buying sex are **illegal** under South African law. In addition, related activities—such as public solicitation, brothel-keeping, and living off the earnings of prostitution—are also criminal offenses.
- Economic hardship, unemployment, and gender inequality push many—especially women from marginalized backgrounds—into sex work as a means of survival.
- The country is a source, transit, and destination for trafficking, with women and children being the most affected.
- An estimated 60% of sex workers in South Africa are HIV positive, with rates as high as 71.8% in Johannesburg. The criminalization of sex work restricts access to medical care, encourages risky working conditions, and fuels stigma, worsening public health outcomes.
- Advocacy groups such as SWEAT and the Asijiki Coalition are pushing for decriminalization, arguing it would reduce violence, improve healthcare access, and uphold sex workers' rights. The South African government announced plans to pursue decriminalization in 2022, but no legal changes have been implemented yet.

CHAPTER 8
LGBTQ

IN THIS CHAPTER

- Homophobia in South Africa
- LGBTQ Legislation
- LGBTQ Tourism and Safety Concerns
- General Questions
- Law of the Land True Story
- Law of the Land Hypothetical

CHAPTER 8

LGBTQ

Homophobia in South Africa

South Africa's 1996 post-apartheid constitution was a global milestone—it was **the first to explicitly ban discrimination based on sexual orientation.** This groundbreaking inclusion came largely due to the activism of figures like Simon Nkoli and Beverley Ditsie, who linked the struggle for LGBTQ+ rights with broader human rights movements during the anti-apartheid era. Despite the progressive legal turn, apartheid-era laws had criminalized same-sex relationships and entrenched homophobia, effects of which persist in social attitudes today. The ruling African National Congress embraced formal equality after 1994, but implementation and cultural change have been inconsistent.

Legal protections for LGBTQ+ individuals are robust on paper, but societal acceptance is deeply uneven. Major cities such as Johannesburg, Cape Town, and Durban are more inclusive, supporting Pride events and LGBTQ+ venues. However, in rural provinces and townships, conservative values often dominate, and visible queerness can provoke hostility. Surveys reflect this divide: about 51–67% of South Africans support LGBTQ+ legal equality, but as many as 70% still consider same-sex relationships morally unacceptable. This contradiction illustrates how legal change has outpaced social transformation.

Cultural beliefs often portray LGBTQ+ identities as "un-African" or incompatible with traditional family and gender roles. This misconception is reinforced by religious conservatism. Many Christian and Muslim leaders preach against homosexuality, and some churches actively exclude LGBTQ+ members. However, there are also progressive faith leaders and communities that promote inclusion. Colonial and apartheid-era laws criminalizing homosexuality have also left a lasting legacy, embedding shame and secrecy into many communities' views on sexual orientation and gender diversity. Rigid gender norms further marginalize people who do not conform to masculine or feminine expectations.

Homophobic attitudes appear across many parts of daily life. In the workplace, LGBTQ+ employees face both **overt discrimination and subtle exclusion**—being passed over for promotions, enduring slurs, or lacking supportive policies. In schools, LGBTQ+ youth are often **bullied by peers and ignored by teachers**, leading to poor academic performance and mental health issues. At home, many are **rejected by family**, leading to homelessness or forced conformity. In the media, LGBTQ+ representation has improved, especially in TV dramas and social media, but this visibility is often met with backlash and hate speech, especially online.

Anti-LGBTQ+ violence remains a major issue. In 2021 alone, at least 24 LGBTQ+ South Africans were murdered in hate-motivated attacks. Around 44% report regular experiences of discrimination—verbal abuse, exclusion, and physical or sexual violence. Lesbian and bisexual women, as well as trans and gender-nonconforming people, face disproportionate levels of sexual violence, including so-called **"corrective rape."** Victims often distrust or fear law enforcement, as police are reported to harass, ridicule, or ignore LGBTQ+ complainants. Economic inequality is also pronounced: gender-nonconforming LGBTQ+ people earn, on average, 30% less than heterosexual, gender-conforming men.

South Africa has a number of outspoken LGBTQ+ advocates and allies. **Simon Nkoli**, a Black gay anti-apartheid activist, is remembered for linking race and gay struggles. **Beverley Ditsie**, a filmmaker and co-founder of Africa's first Pride March, continues to campaign for visibility and safety. **Steve Letsike**, founder of the advocacy group Access Chapter 2, now serves in Parliament and champions LGBTQ+ legislation. **President Cyril Ramaphosa** has publicly affirmed LGBTQ+ rights and called for inclusive policies, though critics argue enforcement under his administration remains weak.

LGBTQ Legislation

South Africa has some of the most **supportive and progressive LGBTQ+ laws in the world**, especially compared to other African nations. Its legal framework strongly protects LGBTQ+ rights, though implementation often lags behind. The key laws include:

- **Constitutional Protection (1996):** South Africa's post-apartheid constitution was the **first globally** to prohibit discrimination based on sexual orientation (Section 9). This laid the foundation for LGBTQ+ rights in all areas of life.
- **Decriminalization of Same-Sex Activity (1998):** The Constitutional Court struck down sodomy laws, making same-sex sexual activity legal.
- **Civil Union Act (2006):** Legalized **same-sex marriage**, making South Africa the **first country in Africa** and the **fifth globally** to do so.
- **Adoption Rights (2002 onward):** Same-sex couples can **jointly adopt** children and have full **parental rights**.
- **Gender Identity Recognition (2003):** Under the **Alteration of Sex Description and Sex Status Act**, transgender individuals can legally change their gender marker with supporting medical documentation.
- **Employment Equity Act (1998):** Prohibits discrimination based on sexual orientation in hiring, firing, and working conditions.
- **Hate Speech and Hate Crimes Bill (2024):** Recently enacted to criminalize hate speech and acts of violence targeting people based on **sexual orientation, gender identity, or intersex status.**

Despite these robust legal protections, there are still **gaps and challenges in enforcement**. For example, some civil servants may refuse to officiate same-sex marriages on religious grounds, limiting access to equal marriage rights in more conservative or rural areas. Furthermore, although laws exist on paper, LGBTQ+ people often experience discrimination and violence due to inconsistent enforcement, police inaction, and deep-seated cultural and religious opposition. While gender identity is legally recognized, explicit protections for transgender and non-binary individuals in sectors such as healthcare and education remain incomplete. Overall, South Africa's legal framework is highly supportive, but social implementation remains uneven and continues to require advocacy and reform.

LGBTQ Tourism and Safety Concerns

LGBTQ tourism is **relatively well developed** in South Africa, especially in cities like Cape Town and Johannesburg. **Cape Town**, in particular, is **widely regarded as the LGBTQ capital of Africa.** It offers a well-established LGBTQ+ scene with gay-friendly accommodations, bars, clubs, beaches (such as Clifton 3rd Beach), and annual events like **Cape Town Pride** and the **Mother City Queer Project**. The city actively markets itself as an LGBTQ+ destination and is home to many inclusive businesses and hospitality services. Johannesburg also hosts a large and vibrant Pride parade and has a number of gay-friendly venues in areas like Melville and Rosebank.

Tolerance and acceptance, however, vary sharply by region. Urban areas like Cape Town, Johannesburg, and Durban are generally more LGBTQ-friendly, with greater legal awareness, cultural diversity, and visible LGBTQ+ communities. In contrast, rural provinces and townships can be less tolerant due to deeply rooted cultural and religious conservatism. LGBTQ+ travelers are advised to exercise discretion in these areas, particularly regarding public displays of affection, which may draw unwanted attention or provoke hostility. Public displays of affection between same-sex couples are generally accepted in major cities and tourist hotspots, especially in LGBTQ-welcoming spaces. However, outside of these areas, such behavior may be met with disapproval or harassment. **Caution is advised when traveling in more conservative communities,** where visible signs of queerness may be stigmatized or misunderstood.

While South Africa has strong legal protections for LGBTQ+ individuals, **safety concerns still exist.** Homophobic violence and harassment, including hate crimes, continue to occur, particularly in townships and less developed regions. Visitors are encouraged to stay informed, avoid isolated areas at night, and use LGBTQ-friendly accommodations and services when possible. Despite these concerns, thousands of LGBTQ+ tourists visit South Africa each year and enjoy safe, welcoming experiences—particularly when staying within cosmopolitan or tourist-centered areas.

General Questions

1. ***Are there any specific safety precautions LGBTQ+ travelers should take when visiting South Africa?*** Yes. LGBTQ+ travelers should exercise caution, especially in rural or less developed areas, where homophobic attitudes may be more prevalent. It's advisable to avoid public displays of affection in these regions, as they may attract unwanted attention. Staying in LGBTQ-friendly accommodations, using trusted transportation, and avoiding isolated areas at night are important precautions. Travelers should also be aware of local laws and know where to find support in case of any issues related to discrimination or harassment.

2. ***How well do South African law enforcement agencies handle hate crimes against LGBTQ+ individuals, especially in rural areas?*** Law enforcement in South Africa struggles to effectively address hate crimes against LGBTQ+ individuals, particularly in rural areas. While the country has laws to protect LGBTQ+ people, there are often gaps in enforcement, and many cases of violence or discrimination go unreported or are not properly investigated. In rural areas, where conservative views are more common, LGBTQ+ individuals may face greater challenges in seeking protection, and police may be less responsive to incidents of hate crimes.

Law of the Land True Story[34]

The tragic killing of Muhsin Hendricks, the first openly gay Muslim imam, in South Africa in February 2025, has raised significant concerns about the safety of LGBTQ+ individuals, particularly those advocating for inclusivity and rights. Hendricks, who founded a mosque for gay Muslims and advocated for their acceptance within Islam, was shot in what many believe was an assassination linked to his progressive teachings. His death highlights the persistent risks faced by LGBTQ+ individuals in the country, despite South Africa's legal protections.

While the country's constitution offers strong protections for LGBTQ+ rights, violence and discrimination remain prevalent, especially in rural and conservative areas. Hendricks had previously reported threats and fatwas against him for his stance on LGBTQ+ inclusion, and the Muslim community's stance on homosexuality has long been a point of contention. The incident underscores the broader challenges LGBTQ+ activists and individuals face in South Africa, where acceptance remains uneven, and homophobic violence is still a serious concern.

This event also amplifies concerns for LGBTQ+ tourists visiting South Africa, as visible LGBTQ+ identities and advocacy can attract hostility, especially in more conservative regions. Despite the country's progressive legal framework, the safety and security of LGBTQ+ individuals—both locals and visitors—are threatened by ongoing prejudice and hate crimes, making it crucial for the LGBTQ+ community to remain vigilant and cautious when traveling or engaging in public displays of affection.

34 https://apnews.com/article/gay-imam-muslim-south-africa-lgbtq-fd7db9a1ea53ea039d35fe21a1ff80c9

Law of the Land Hypothetical

HYPOTHETICAL: *Alex, a gay man, is living in Johannesburg and has been in a committed relationship with Chris for two years. They both work in a corporate office where they have not openly expressed their relationship. Alex is considering asking Chris to move in with him, but they are concerned about potential legal issues, especially regarding the recognition of their rights as a same-sex couple. Are Alex and Chris legally protected as a same-sex couple in South Africa, and do they have any legal rights regarding cohabitation, discrimination at work, or the ability to make decisions for one another in case of an emergency?*

ANSWER: *Yes. In South Africa, same-sex couples have significant legal protections. The country's constitution prohibits discrimination based on sexual orientation, and same-sex marriage has been legal since 2006 under the Civil Union Act. As a couple, Alex and Chris have the right to cohabit and share property. They are also protected from workplace discrimination, and their employer cannot discriminate based on their sexual orientation. In the case of an emergency, they can grant one another the right to make medical decisions if both individuals are legally recognized partners, though it would be advisable to formalize this with legal documents like a power of attorney. Overall, their relationship is legally protected, and they have the same rights as heterosexual couples under South African law.*

CHAPTER 9

SEXUALLY MOTIVATED/ VIOLENT CRIMES

IN THIS CHAPTER

- Overview
- Related Legislation
- General Questions
- Law of the Land True Story
- Takeaways

CHAPTER 9

SEXUALLY MOTIVATED/ VIOLENT CRIMES

Overview

Sexually motivated crimes are **highly prevalent** in South Africa, which is known to have some of the highest rates of sexual violence in the world. According to research cited by Ballard Brief, about 28% of South African men admitted to having committed rape, and 46% of those were repeat offenders. Despite government reforms and advocacy, there has only been a modest 6% decrease in rape rates since 1996. In the third quarter of the 2024/2025 financial year, official statistics reported a 3% year-over-year decline in rape and attempted sexual offenses, but cases of sexual assault increased, with most incidents taking place in domestic settings.[35]

The high incidence of sexual violence in South Africa is rooted in a range of social, cultural, and economic factors. Deeply entrenched **patriarchal norms** and **rigid gender roles** foster a culture where women and children are seen as subordinate, and violence is sometimes used as a form of control or punishment. **Economic hardship** and widespread poverty exacerbate the issue, leaving many women vulnerable due to dependency or lack of escape options. Cultural myths such as the **"virgin cleansing"**

35 https://apnews.com/article/south-africa-rape-protest-violence-women-5442fd87789ee6251254a1df5024e096

myth—which falsely claims that sex with a virgin can cure disease—also perpetuate harmful behaviors. On top of this, the criminal justice system frequently fails survivors; law enforcement and judicial responses are often under-resourced, slow, or biased, which contributes to a sense of impunity for perpetrators.

Women and girls are the most affected demographic, with sub-Saharan Africa—particularly South Africa—showing high rates of sexual abuse during childhood. UNICEF estimates that over 79 million girls and women in the region have experienced rape or sexual assault before age 18. Children are frequent victims of kidnapping and abuse, and LGBTQ+ individuals are also disproportionately targeted, facing extreme violence including so-called "corrective rape," where sexual assault is used as a tool to enforce heterosexuality.[36]

Related Legislation[37]

South Africa has a relatively comprehensive legal framework for addressing sexually motivated crimes, but **enforcement remains inconsistent** due to social and institutional challenges. The primary law governing these crimes is the **Criminal Law (Sexual Offences and Related Matters) Amendment Act of 2007** (commonly known as **SORMAA**), which significantly broadened the legal definitions of sexual offenses. It recognizes both men and women as potential victims and includes a wide range of offenses such as **rape, sexual assault, compelled sexual acts**, and **exploitation**. The Act mandates the reporting of child sexual abuse and establishes the **National Register for Sex Offenders (NRSO)**, which contains the names of individuals convicted of sexual crimes against vulnerable persons, including children and individuals with mental disabilities.[38]

36 https://www.sciencedirect.com/science/article/pii/S0145213422005154

37 https://www.legalwise.co.za/help-yourself/legal-articles/gender-based-violence-stricter-legislation-its-way-prevent-and-protect#~

38 https://www.justice.gov.za/vg/nrso.html

Complementing this law is **the Criminal Law Amendment Act of 1997,** which introduced **mandatory minimum sentences** for serious crimes, including rape. For a first offense of rape, the minimum sentence is **fifteen years,** escalating to **twenty years for a second offense** and **twenty-five years or life imprisonment for a third offense or cases involving aggravating factors** such as gang rape or where the perpetrator knowingly transmits HIV. **Sexual assault,** a charge distinct from rape, can carry a sentence **of up to ten years. Offenses against children or mentally disabled persons** often result in sentences at the higher end of the spectrum, sometimes **life imprisonment.** The law also criminalizes the possession, production, or distribution of child pornography, with penalties of up to ten years or a fine.

The **Children's Act of 2005** and the **Domestic Violence Act of 1998** provide further protections by prohibiting abuse and exploitation and enabling victims to obtain protection orders. The Children's Act also compels certain professionals to report suspected abuse. In the context of domestic abuse, the legal framework defines sexual abuse broadly and supports victims with protective remedies such as interdicts and court orders.

Enforcement is carried out by **specialized units** within the South African Police Service, particularly the **Family Violence, Child Protection,** and **Sexual Offences (FCS) Units.** These units are supported by the **Thuthuzela Care Centres (TCCs),** which are multidisciplinary facilities run in cooperation with the National Prosecuting Authority. TCCs are designed to provide survivors with immediate medical attention, post-exposure prophylaxis for HIV, psychological counseling, and legal assistance in one location. Prosecutors with expertise in sexual offense cases are assigned to work on these matters, and survivors can testify via closed-circuit television or behind screens to reduce secondary trauma.

Despite this strong legal framework, enforcement remains problematic. **Conviction rates are low;** according to Statistics South Africa, only around 8.6% of reported rape cases result in a conviction. Challenges include police inefficiency, lack of sensitivity training, forensic backlogs, and societal stigma that leads to underreporting. Victims frequently withdraw cases due to poor treatment by law enforcement or delays in prosecution.

Recent legislative reforms, introduced in 2021, have attempted to address some of these weaknesses. These include three **Gender-Based Violence Amendment Bills** which expanded the National Register for Sex Offenders to include broader categories of offenders, **tightened bail conditions** for those accused of sexual crimes, and **broadened the definition of domestic violence** to include spiritual, emotional, and technological abuse.

General Questions

1. ***Do laws in South Africa related to sex crimes protect the victims equally?*** **No.** While South African laws are written to protect all victims equally, in practice, this is not always the case. Marginalized groups such as LGBTQ+ individuals, sex workers, and people in poor communities often face discrimination, weak police response, or stigma, which limits their access to justice. The legal framework is inclusive, but unequal enforcement results in gaps in protection.

2. ***How are foreign visitors protected in cases of sexual assault?*** Foreign visitors in South Africa are protected by the same sexual offense laws as citizens. If assaulted, they can report the crime at any police station and are entitled to medical care, post-exposure prophylaxis (PEP) for HIV, counseling, and a forensic exam. However, despite these protections, foreign victims may face difficulties such as language barriers, fear of mistreatment, or uncertainty about how the system works. Embassies and consulates can assist by providing information, interpreters, and referrals to legal or medical services. The law does not discriminate by nationality, but actual access can depend on location and available resources.

3. ***Pursuant to law, what is the age of consent for sex in South Africa?*** The age of consent is 16 years old. Engaging in sexual activity with someone under 16 is considered statutory rape, even if the minor consents. However, if both parties are between 12 and 16, or if there's an age difference of less than two years between them, no criminal charges will be filed; instead, they may be sent for counseling.

Law of the Land True Story[39]

In April 2025, a large crowd gathered in Pretoria to protest against gender-based violence following the alleged rape of a 7-year-old girl, known as Cwecwe for anonymity. The incident, which occurred at her school last year, was only reported a month later, igniting outrage across the nation. The protest was part of a broader outcry, with demonstrations also taking place in Cape Town and Matatiele.

Protesters, mostly dressed in black, carried placards condemning the widespread issue of sexual violence against women and children. Many, including reigning Miss South Africa, Mia le Roux, expressed their frustration with the justice system, which they feel has failed victims. Le Roux emphasized the urgent need for action, calling gender-based violence a "natural disaster."

The victim's mother has been vocal in her disappointment with the lack of timely response, highlighting the need for the government to declare gender-based violence a national crisis. Other speakers, such as Nobuntu Hlazo-Webster, a political leader, called for drastic measures, including declaring a state of emergency and publishing the sex offender registry to protect vulnerable individuals from repeat offenders. While crime statistics have shown a slight decrease in rape cases, there has been an increase in sexual assault incidents. A significant number of these crimes occur in domestic settings, with homes, public

39 https://apnews.com/article/south-africa-rape-protest-violence-women-5442fd87789ee6251254a1df5024e096

spaces, and institutions like schools and nightclubs being common sites of violence.

Takeaways

- South Africa has one of the highest rates of sexual violence in the world, with studies indicating that a significant proportion of men have admitted to committing rape, and many are repeat offenders.
- Deeply rooted patriarchal norms, economic hardship, and harmful cultural myths contribute to the high incidence of gender-based violence in the country.
- South Africa has a comprehensive legal framework, including the SORMAA and the Children's Act, aimed at protecting victims of sexual violence. The legal framework is inclusive of both men and women, and there are provisions for mandatory reporting of child abuse and establishment of sex offender registries.
- Despite the strong legal framework, enforcement is inconsistent. The criminal justice system faces significant barriers, including police inefficiency, forensic backlogs, and societal stigma that often leads to underreporting and a low conviction rate for rape cases.
- In 2021, reforms were introduced to address gender-based violence, including expanding the National Register for Sex Offenders, tightening bail conditions for accused individuals, and broadening the definition of domestic violence. However, challenges in enforcement and societal attitudes still hinder progress in reducing sexual violence.

CHAPTER 10

ARRESTED IN SOUTH AFRICA

IN THIS CHAPTER

- Overview
- The Arrest Process
- Rights of the Arrested Person
- Getting Legal Assistance
- Bail
- Complaints Against the Police
- General Questions

CHAPTER 10

ARRESTED IN SOUTH AFRICA

Overview

When traveling in a foreign country, it's imperative to recognize that you are subject to the legal jurisdiction and regulations of that nation. These laws may significantly differ from those in your home country and might not offer the same legal protections you are accustomed to. It's crucial to bear in mind that penalties for violating foreign laws can be more severe than those for similar offenses in your home country, and ignorance of these laws is not typically accepted as a defense.

The consequences for breaking the law while abroad can be severe and may include expulsion, fines, arrest, or imprisonment. Even unintentional violations can lead to serious legal repercussions. It is essential for travelers to be aware of and adhere to the laws of the host country to avoid legal entanglements and ensure a safe and enjoyable experience. Specifically, stringent penalties are often enforced for possession, use, or trafficking of illegal drugs in many countries. Convicted offenders can expect severe consequences, including lengthy jail sentences and hefty fines. The legal processes for foreigners in the event of an arrest abroad involve being charged or indicted, prosecuted, potentially convicted and sentenced, and, if applicable, going through an appeals process.

Navigating a foreign legal system can be complex, and individuals arrested abroad must be prepared to comply with the legal procedures of the host country. Seeking legal representation and understanding the local legal nuances are crucial steps for those facing legal issues in a foreign jurisdiction.

Awareness of and adherence to the laws of a foreign country are paramount when traveling. Understanding the potential consequences for legal violations and being prepared to navigate the legal system of the host country are essential aspects of responsible international travel.

The Arrest Process[40]

In South Africa, the arrest process follows a clear legal framework, specifically the **Constitution** and the **Criminal Procedure Act** (**CPA**) **of 1977,** to ensure the rights of both local citizens and foreign nationals are protected. Common criminal charges in South Africa include **theft, assault, fraud, drug-related offenses,** and **immigration violations.**

An arrest typically begins when the South African Police Service (SAPS) has reasonable grounds to suspect that a person has committed a crime. In many cases, the police must obtain an **arrest warrant** from a magistrate or judge, which requires sufficient evidence linking the suspect to the crime. However, a warrant is not needed if the person is caught in the act (in flagrante delicto), if there's a risk they will flee, or if the offense is classified as "schedule 1" (e.g., rape, murder, robbery, or certain drug offenses).

Once the arrest is made, the officer must clearly inform the person that they are under arrest, explain the reason for the arrest, and advise them of their constitutional rights, including the right to remain silent and the right to legal representation. The arrestee must be handled with dignity and without the use of unnecessary force. If a foreign national is arrested, they also have the right to contact their embassy or consulate.

After the arrest, the individual is taken into custody and detained at a police station. Within 48 hours—excluding weekends and public

40 https://www.arrivealive.mobi/standard-operating-procedures-for-arrest-and-detention

holidays—the person must appear before a magistrate's court for a bail hearing. At this hearing, the court decides whether to release the accused pending trial and under what conditions. If the charge is serious, the court may deny bail or require a formal bail application.

If the case proceeds, the suspect is either remanded in custody or released on bail until the next court date. Meanwhile, the police and prosecution will investigate further and prepare for trial. If the case is weak or the prosecution decides not to proceed, charges may be dropped, and the suspect released. Throughout this process, both citizens and foreigners have the right to humane treatment, legal support, and a fair judicial process.

Rights of the Arrested Person[41]

In South Africa, the rights of arrested individuals are firmly rooted in the **Constitution** and enforced through various legal statutes and judicial practices. According to Section 35 of the Constitution, every arrested person has the **right to remain silent** and **to be informed promptly of the reason for their arrest**. They must be told that anything they say may be used against them in court. They are entitled to **legal representation** and, if they cannot afford an attorney, the state must provide one at no cost. Arrested individuals also have the **right to challenge the lawfulness of their detention** and to appear before a court **within 48 hours**. The courts must ensure that detention is justified and that due process is followed. Additionally, arrested persons must be **detained under humane conditions**, with access to food, water, medical treatment, and communication with their family and legal counsel.

For foreign nationals, South Africa's legal protections are generally the same as for citizens, but there are additional layers of complexity. Foreigners have the right to **consular access**, meaning they can request that their embassy or consulate be notified of their arrest. This is crucial, as embassies can provide legal resources, interpreters, and liaison

41 https://criminaldefenceattorney.co.za/2025/03/17/your-rights-when-arrested/

services. However, foreign nationals may be asked to **prove their legal status in the country**. If they cannot, they may be detained for immigration violations and could face deportation proceedings in addition to criminal charges. Language barriers, unfamiliarity with South African legal procedures, and fear of mistreatment can all hinder foreigners' ability to assert their rights. Therefore, **prompt consular involvement and legal representation are vital to ensure they receive fair treatment under the law.**

Getting Legal Assistance

In South Africa, everyone—regardless of nationality—has the constitutional right to legal representation if arrested or charged with a criminal offense. This is guaranteed under Section 35 of the South African Constitution, which affirms that every detained person has the right to choose and consult with a legal practitioner, and if they cannot afford one, to be assigned a legal representative at state expense.

The **Legal Aid South Africa** organization provides state-funded attorneys to qualifying individuals who cannot afford private legal services. If arrested, a foreigner should immediately request to speak with a lawyer and notify the arresting officer of their nationality. According to international consular agreements and South African law, foreign nationals also have the right to contact their embassy or consulate without delay. Police must facilitate this communication.

If you are arrested in South Africa, the first steps should be to remain calm, clearly assert your right to remain silent, and immediately request access to a lawyer. Avoid signing any statements or answering substantive questions until you have legal counsel present. **Inform the police that you are a foreign national and request that your embassy or consulate be notified.** It is important to document as much as possible and request the names and badge numbers of the arresting officers, which can be useful for later legal or diplomatic action.

Your embassy's role is primarily advisory and diplomatic. While they cannot interfere with South Africa's judicial process, they can advocate for fair treatment, provide a list of approved local attorneys, assist with communication to family members, and, in some cases, monitor the legal process to ensure due process is followed. In high-profile or sensitive cases, embassy officials may also attend court proceedings or liaise with South African authorities on the detainee's behalf.

Foreign nationals who cannot afford private legal representation are not left without options. Several well-established organizations provide **free or low-cost legal aid** specifically designed to help vulnerable individuals, including migrants, refugees, asylum seekers, and undocumented people. The cornerstone of the country's legal aid system is **Legal Aid South Africa**, a state-funded institution mandated to provide legal representation to those who meet certain financial thresholds. While many of its clients are South African citizens, Legal Aid SA also assists **foreign nationals**, particularly in criminal cases or where fundamental human rights are at risk. Foreigners can approach their nearest Legal Aid office—often located within Magistrate's Courts—to apply for help, and their eligibility is determined through a **means test** assessing income and assets.

More information and office locations are available on their website at **https://legal-aid.co.za**.

In addition to government aid, **ProBono.Org** plays a vital role in connecting indigent individuals with private lawyers who volunteer their services. This nonprofit organization has offices in Johannesburg, Durban, and Cape Town and is known for its strong advocacy on behalf of refugees, asylum seekers, victims of domestic violence, and migrant workers. It handles a wide array of cases, from **family law to labor disputes**, and is particularly responsive to the legal challenges foreign nationals often face.

For more information, please visit their website at **https://probono.org.za**.

For legal issues that directly relate to **immigration status, detention**, and **refugee rights, Lawyers for Human Rights** (**LHR**) offers a specialized program known as the **Refugee and Migrant Rights Programme**. Their services are geared specifically toward non-citizens, offering legal assistance for those facing deportation, wrongful detention, or the complexities of refugee status determination. LHR is a long-standing advocate in this space and has successfully defended the rights of many non-nationals across South Africa.[42]

The **Scalabrini Centre of Cape Town** is another important resource for migrants. Though it does not take criminal cases, its **Advocacy Programme** provides free legal help for issues like **visa renewals, documentation problems, labor exploitation**, and **access to public services**. The center is especially helpful to those who are new to the country and unsure of how to navigate South Africa's legal and administrative systems.[43]

Lastly, **university-based law clinics**, such as those at the University of Cape Town (UCT), the University of the Witwatersrand (Wits), and the University of Pretoria (UP), often represent foreign nationals in both civil and criminal matters. Staffed by law students under the supervision of qualified attorneys, these clinics provide a valuable training ground for future lawyers while offering much-needed support to people who can't afford a private defense. UCT's law clinic, for example, offers comprehensive legal services to non-citizens as long as they qualify for assistance.[44]

Together, these organizations form a patchwork of support for foreigners in need of legal help in South Africa. Whether a person is detained at a police station, facing a labor dispute, or trying to regularize their immigration status, there are **multiple pathways to free legal counsel**. However, early action is critical—seeking assistance as soon as possible increases the likelihood of receiving adequate legal protection.

---

42 https://www.lhr.org.za

43 https://www.scalabrini.org.za

44 https://law.uct.ac.za/law/law-clinic

Bail[45]

South Africa maintains a **structured bail system** governed primarily by the Criminal Procedure Act, 51 of 1977, which outlines the legal framework for granting and regulating bail, a legal mechanism that allows an arrested person to be released from custody while awaiting trial, on the condition that they return to court when required. The decision to grant bail is based on several factors, including the **seriousness of the offense**, the **risk of flight**, the **interests of justice**, and the **likelihood of interfering** with witnesses or evidence.

There are **three types of bail** in South Africa: police bail, prosecutor's bail, and court-ordered bail. Police bail is available for **minor, schedule 1 offenses** (like petty theft) and can be **granted by the arresting officer** at the police station. **Prosecutor's bail** applies to slightly **more serious offenses** and requires the involvement of **the public prosecutor**. In both cases, the accused can be released within hours if bail is approved and paid. For more **serious or schedule 5 and 6 crimes** (e.g., rape, armed robbery, or murder), bail can only be granted by a **magistrate** or **judge in court**, typically after a **formal bail hearing.** The accused may need to prove that exceptional circumstances exist which justify their release.

Bail amounts vary significantly depending on the charge and the accused's personal circumstances. Courts may set a **cash amount**, but **non-financial conditions** are also common—such as surrendering a passport, reporting regularly to a police station, or not contacting witnesses. Failure to comply can lead to **forfeiture of bail money** and **re-arrest**.

For **foreign visitors**, courts are generally more cautious when considering bail due to the perceived **flight risk.** Judges may require additional safeguards, such as **higher bail amounts**, the **surrender of travel documents**, or even **guarantees from local contacts.** While foreigners have the same legal right to apply for bail, they are more likely to face **strict conditions** or even **detention** until trial in serious cases. That said,

45 https://www.martinvermaak.co.za/how-to-get-bail-in-south-africa-a-complete-guide

consular officials can advocate for their nationals, help explain legal rights and sometimes assist in arranging legal representation or surety for bail.

Complaints Against the Police[46]

The South African Police Service (SAPS) has a **complex and often criticized public image**, with a reputation that ranges from dedicated service in some areas to widespread concerns about corruption, brutality, and inefficiency in others. In many communities, especially those affected by poverty or high crime rates, trust in the police is low. Officers are frequently accused of misconduct, and allegations of abuse of power are not uncommon. Public confidence has also been undermined by repeated incidents where police have failed to respond adequately to serious crimes such as domestic violence and sexual assault.

The most common complaints lodged against SAPS include the use of **excessive force, unlawful detention**, and **police brutality** during arrests or crowd control operations. **Corruption** is another major concern, with reports of officers soliciting bribes in exchange for dropping charges or avoiding arrest. Many individuals also report being **arrested without proper cause or warrants**, and detainees sometimes experience **poor treatment while in custody**, including lack of medical care or access to legal representation. In addition, there have been numerous reports of **police negligence**—such as ignoring reports of violent crimes—or mistreating foreign nationals, particularly refugees, migrants, and asylum seekers.

Individuals who believe they have been mistreated by the police can file a formal complaint with the Independent Police Investigative Directorate (IPID), which is tasked with investigating serious misconduct by SAPS members, including deaths in custody, assaults, and corruption.

46 https://theconversation.com/south-africans-have-low-trust-in-their-police-heres-why-17882

Complaints can be submitted in person, by email, or online through IPID's official website at **https://www.gov.za/about-government/contact-directory/departments/independent-police-investigative-directorate-ipid.**

The Civilian Secretariat for Police Service also receives complaints and provides oversight on broader policy and accountability matters, although it does not conduct investigations directly.[47]

In cases involving violations of constitutional or human rights—such as discrimination, torture, or unlawful imprisonment—the South African Human Rights Commission (SAHRC) can step in to assist, and complaints can be submitted through their website at **https://www.sahrc.org.za.**

For individuals who need legal assistance to pursue complaints, particularly those involving police abuse, organizations such as **the Legal Resources Centre**[48] and **Lawyers for Human Rights**[49] offer legal aid and support. These groups are particularly helpful for foreign nationals who may face additional challenges such as language barriers, legal uncertainty, or fear of retaliation. Although the process of holding police accountable in South Africa can be slow and difficult, these mechanisms and organizations provide essential support for those seeking justice.

47 https://www.policesecretariat.gov.za

48 https://www.lrc.org.za

49 https://www.lhr.org.za

General Questions

1. ***If I am convicted in South Africa, am I likely to be released on bail pending the outcome of my appeal?*** In South Africa, it is possible to be released on bail while appealing a conviction, but it's not guaranteed. The court considers factors like the seriousness of the offense, flight risk, and the likelihood of a successful appeal. Since the presumption of innocence no longer applies, getting post-conviction bail is more difficult than before trial. If you followed bail conditions during trial, that may help your case. Foreign nationals often face extra scrutiny due to flight risk and may be required to meet stricter conditions, such as surrendering passports or checking in regularly with authorities.

2. ***Who is entitled to bail?*** In South Africa, anyone accused of a crime is generally entitled to apply for bail, but the court decides whether to grant it based on the specifics of the case. For less serious offenses, bail is more likely to be granted quickly. However, for serious crimes like murder, rape, or drug trafficking, the accused must convince the court that their release is in the interest of justice. The court evaluates factors like the risk of flight, potential interference with witnesses, danger to the public, and likelihood of reoffending.

3. ***If I am arrested, how soon will I see a judge or magistrate?*** If you are arrested in South Africa, the law requires that you be brought before a judge or magistrate **within 48 hours of your arrest.** If the arrest happens over a weekend or public holiday, the 48-hour period excludes non-court days, meaning you must appear in court on the next working day. This first appearance is typically for a bail hearing or to inform you of the charges, and it's your legal right to have this hearing without unnecessary delay.

4. ***What should I do if I believe I've been wrongfully arrested in South Africa?*** If you believe you've been wrongfully arrested in South Africa, stay calm and do not resist. Make sure you assert your legal rights to legal representation and to contact your embassy or consulate. If you believe that the arrest was unlawful, you may later file a civil claim or lodge a complaint with the Independent Police Investigative Directorate (IPID).

CHAPTER 11

JAILS VS. PRISONS: CONDITIONS & CULTURE

IN THIS CHAPTER

- Overview
- Prison Conditions and Living Environments
- Inmate Rights and Legal Protections
- General Questions

CHAPTER 11

JAILS VS. PRISONS: CONDITIONS & CULTURE

Overview

Like in most countries, in South Africa, the criminal justice system distinguishes between **jails**—used mainly for **pre-trial detention or short-term sentences**—and **prisons**, which house those serving **longer-term sentences**. Both are operated by **the Department of Correctional Services (DCS)**, though holding cells at police stations may be used for very short stays during the initial arrest phase. South African prisons have long faced **severe overcrowding,** with many facilities operating far beyond their intended capacity. This leads to strained resources, poor sanitation, insufficient healthcare, and heightened violence, including gang activity and sexual abuse. These conditions are especially hard on vulnerable groups, such as LGBTQ+ inmates, foreign nationals, and juveniles.

Despite the challenges, the government has instituted some **rehabilitation efforts.** These include educational programs, vocational training, psychological counseling, and reintegration support aimed at reducing reoffending. Non-governmental organizations such as NICRO (National Institute for Crime Prevention and the Reintegration of Offenders) also play a role by offering life skills workshops and post-release assistance. However, access to these programs is inconsistent and often limited by funding, staffing shortages, and infrastructure constraints.

Prison Conditions and Living Environment

Prison conditions and the living environment in South Africa are shaped by significant challenges, despite the formal classification and management systems in place. The **Department of Correctional Services (DCS)** administers about **240 prisons** across six regions, organized by **security levels**—minimum, medium, and maximum—and inmates are classified accordingly based on the **nature of their crime, behavior**, and **sentence length.** However, overcrowding often undermines this classification, leading to dangerous mixing of high-risk and vulnerable inmates, including juveniles and non-violent offenders.

Access to health care in South African prisons is **a persistent concern.** While basic medical services are theoretically available within facilities, in practice, they are often understaffed, under-resourced, and slow to respond to serious health issues. Chronic illnesses like HIV/AIDS and tuberculosis are widespread among the prison population, and mental health services are limited. Delays in diagnosis, treatment, and referrals are common, sometimes resulting in preventable deaths.

Basic needs such as **food, hygiene**, and **sanitation** are also **frequently compromised.** Meals are provided but are often nutritionally inadequate, poorly prepared, or served inconsistently. Clean water and toiletries are in short supply in many facilities, and overcrowded, unsanitary cells contribute to health risks. Inmates often rely on their families or outside donors to provide basic items, which can lead to disparities among prisoners. Overall, while there are official standards, the reality for many prisoners in South Africa falls far short due to budget constraints, infrastructure decay, and administrative challenges.

Inmate Rights and Legal Protections

In South Africa, prisoners retain many of their constitutional rights despite being incarcerated. According to Section 35 of the South African Constitution, all detainees and sentenced prisoners have the **right to be treated with dignity and humanity,** and not to be subjected to torture or cruel, inhuman, or degrading treatment. These rights also include access to adequate medical care, communication with family and legal representatives, and the right to challenge the legality of their detention.

Inmates are entitled to **access legal resources** and pursue court appeals if they believe their conviction or sentencing was unjust. **Legal aid** is available to prisoners who cannot afford private counsel, and they can file appeals or motions through the court system (See Chapter 10). However, systemic delays and the limited availability of legal support within prisons can hinder timely access to justice. Some inmates rely on legal NGOs or assistance from family members to pursue their cases effectively.

Abuse and mistreatment in prisons remain ongoing concerns. Reports of physical violence by prison officials or other inmates, psychological abuse, and neglect are not uncommon. Inmates who experience abuse can report the matter to the **Judicial Inspectorate for Correctional Services** (JICS), an oversight body tasked with monitoring prison conditions and investigating complaints. However, many prisoners hesitate to report abuse due to fear of retaliation or lack of trust in the system's response. While legal avenues exist for recourse, practical barriers and institutional inefficiencies continue to limit their effectiveness.

General Questions

1. ***Do jails and prisons offer religious services to inmates?* Yes.** Jails and prisons in South Africa generally offer religious services to inmates. Chaplains and religious volunteers from various faiths—primarily Christian denominations, but also including Islam, traditional African religions, and others—are permitted to visit and conduct services, counsel prisoners, and provide religious materials. Participation is voluntary, and inmates have the right to practice their religion as long as it does not disrupt order or security.

2. ***How do prisoners spend their time?*** How prisoners spend their time in South Africa depends on the facility's security level and available resources. Most inmates follow a strict routine that includes headcounts, meals, and scheduled time for exercise. Some participate in labor or vocational programs such as agriculture, laundry, or workshops, while others may have access to educational classes or rehabilitation programs—though these opportunities are often limited by overcrowding and staff shortages. Many prisoners spend long hours in overcrowded cells due to understaffing and lockdowns, which can restrict access to outdoor time and programs.

3. ***What type of jobs can inmates perform?*** In South African prisons, inmates may perform various types of jobs depending on the facility and their security classification. Common work assignments include kitchen duties, cleaning, laundry services, agricultural labor, woodworking, metalwork, and maintenance tasks. Some prisons also operate workshops where inmates produce furniture, clothing, or crafts for internal use or sale. These jobs are intended to support rehabilitation by instilling discipline and providing basic vocational skills, though they are often unpaid or come with only minimal compensation.

4. ***How does the prison commissary system work in South Africa?*** The prison commissary system in South Africa allows inmates to purchase basic goods like toiletries, snacks, and stationery using funds deposited into their prison accounts by family or friends. The selection is limited and varies by facility, and prices may be higher than outside prison. Access to the commissary can be restricted as a disciplinary measure or based on a prisoner's classification. Since most inmates lack financial support, not everyone can benefit from the commissary system equally.

5. ***What type of medical care do prisoners receive?*** Prisoners in South Africa are legally entitled to access healthcare under the Constitution and the Correctional Services Act. Basic medical care is typically provided through on-site prison clinics staffed by nurses and visiting doctors, with more serious cases referred to outside public hospitals. Services include treatment for chronic illnesses like HIV/AIDS and tuberculosis, which are prevalent in the prison population. However, inmates often face long wait times, staff shortages, medication delays, and poor conditions, especially in overcrowded facilities. Mental health services are limited, and psychological care is frequently inadequate for the needs of many inmates.

6. ***What is prison culture in South Africa?*** Prison culture in South Africa is deeply shaped by a combination of overcrowding, gang activity, and hierarchical social dynamics. Gangs have a powerful influence in many prisons, enforcing their own rules and recruiting members, sometimes through coercion. Violence, intimidation, and extortion are common, particularly in overcrowded or poorly supervised facilities. Despite the presence of rehabilitation programs, the harsh environment often reinforces criminal behavior rather than reforming it.

CHAPTER 12

HELPING A FRIEND OR RELATIVE IMPRISONED IN SOUTH AFRICA

IN THIS CHAPTER

- Overview
- Sending Food, Supplies, and Money to an Inmate
- Mail, Phone Calls, and Visitation
- Prison Scams
- Upon Release

CHAPTER 12

HELPING A FRIEND OR RELATIVE IMPRISONED IN SOUTH AFRICA

Overview

If a family member or friend is imprisoned while abroad in South Africa, it's essential to act quickly and follow a few key steps. First, confirm the person's location and the reason for their detention—this can usually be done through direct communication with the arresting police station or correctional facility. As soon as possible, **contact your country's embassy or consulate** in South Africa. Embassies can provide vital support, including verifying the detainee's well-being, offering a list of local English-speaking attorneys, and explaining the legal process. However, embassies cannot interfere in the legal proceedings, get someone out of jail, or pay legal fees.

For U.S. citizens, for example, the **U.S. Embassy in Pretoria** and **consulates in Cape Town, Durban, and Johannesburg** can assist in contacting family back home, ensuring the detainee receives appropriate medical care if needed, and helping them understand their rights under South African law. They can also monitor the conditions of detention to ensure international standards are met.

You can support your relative or friend detained in South Africa in several other ways. Maintaining regular communication is essential—**writing letters or speaking by phone** helps provide emotional stability and keeps them connected to the outside world. Depending on the facility, inmates may also have access to **video calls or email. Financial assistance** can also be crucial. Sending money allows your loved one to purchase food, hygiene items, and other essentials through the prison commissary. This can be done by transferring funds to their inmate account or, for U.S. citizens, through an OCS Trust set up via the embassy.[50]

Sending Food, Supplies, and Money to an Inmate

In South Africa, families and friends cannot directly bring or send cooked food or groceries to inmates in prison. The Department of Correctional Services (DCS) strictly regulates what can be provided to prisoners, and outside food is generally prohibited for security and health reasons. Instead, prisoners receive meals prepared by the prison system, and dietary needs are supposed to be accommodated within the standard prison meal framework.

Packages are also **heavily restricted.** In most cases, inmates are not allowed to receive parcels directly unless there is special permission granted for specific items like clothing, toiletries, or reading materials. These must usually be new, unaltered, and **sent through approved procedures or delivered during designated visiting hours if permitted.** Each correctional facility may have its own set of guidelines and approval processes, and **all items are subject to inspection and approval by the prison authorities.** Prohibited items include electronics, sharp objects, food, or any materials considered a security threat.

Sending money to inmates is possible and **commonly done through deposit systems set up at the prison or via electronic transfer to the prison's account,** where funds are then credited to the inmate's prison trust account. These funds can be used by the inmate to purchase basic items from the prison commissary (canteen), such as snacks, toiletries, and stationery. Visitors can inquire at the facility about the exact banking details, reference format, and limitations on the amount that can be sent.

50 https://usacs-info.com/en-es/topics/us-citizen-arrest/person_in_country_prison_help

Mail, Phone Calls, and Visitation

In South Africa, inmates are allowed to receive and send mail, but **all correspondence is monitored and subject to inspection by prison authorities to prevent the smuggling of contraband or the planning of illegal activities.** Letters must go through official channels, and both incoming and outgoing mail may be delayed due to administrative checks. Inmates are not permitted to receive parcels or printed materials unless authorized.

Inmates are not allowed to possess or use personal cell phones, and possession is considered a serious offense. However, they are allowed to make **monitored phone calls through designated prison telephones.** These calls are typically limited in frequency and duration and can only be made to approved contacts. The number of calls and access varies depending on the security level of the facility and the inmate's behavior. Generally, inmates must request call privileges and provide the names and numbers of intended contacts for approval. All conversations are monitored; only calls to legal representatives may receive some privacy protections.

Visitation in South African prisons is **permitted but strictly regulated.** Typically, only immediate family and approved visitors are allowed. The frequency of visits varies depending on the security classification of the inmate, with sentenced offenders usually allowed visits once or twice a month. Visitors must bring identification, and **all visits must be scheduled in advance.** Physical contact is often limited or prohibited, and visits take place in monitored visiting areas. Visitors are subject to searches, and bringing unauthorized items—including food, electronics, or money—is strictly forbidden. It is highly advisable to contact the prison ahead of time to understand its specific rules, visiting hours, and required procedures.

Prison Scams

Scams related to South African prisons often target families or friends of inmates, as well as the general public. One common scam involves

individuals posing as correctional officials or legal representatives claiming they can secure an inmate's early release or special privileges in exchange for payment. These scammers may contact relatives using information obtained from corrupt insiders or social media, offering fake legal services, visitation access, or promising to improve prison conditions. In some cases, they even impersonate inmates themselves, claiming to need urgent funds for medical treatment, food, or legal fees.

Red flags to watch out for include **unsolicited messages or phone calls** from people claiming to work for the Department of Correctional Services or a legal aid group, especially if they pressure you to act quickly or keep the communication secret. Other warning signs include **vague details, requests for payment through non-official channels** (like money transfer services or personal bank accounts), and **poor spelling or grammar in written messages.** Legitimate prison officials and lawyers will never demand bribes or payment in exchange for services that are either free or legally standardized.

If you suspect a scam, do not send any money or personal information. Instead, **report the incident to the South African Police Service** (SAPS), and **contact the Department of Correctional Services directly to verify any claims.** Families of inmates can also reach out to their embassy or consulate for assistance and verification if they are contacted from inside a South African prison. **Staying cautious and verifying all communication through official channels is key to avoiding these types of fraud.**

Upon Release

Foreigners released from prison or jail in South Africa are typically subject to additional legal obligations and immigration-related procedures. Upon release, **non-citizens are usually transferred to the custody of the Department of Home Affairs,** especially if they were undocumented at the time of arrest or their visa has expired during incarceration. They may be detained further at a repatriation center like Lindela before being deported, depending on the nature of their offense and immigration status. Even for foreigners with valid visas, certain criminal convictions can lead to visa cancellation and a ban on re-entry.

Additional restrictions may include **reporting requirements** if they are released on parole or under supervision, although parole is not always granted to foreigners due to the likelihood of deportation. In some cases, South African authorities may inform the individual's home country or embassy, and coordination may be required for travel arrangements or legal monitoring. Foreign nationals are strongly advised to contact their consulate upon release to clarify their status and get assistance with travel or legal follow-up. **Remaining in the country without valid immigration status after release can result in detention and re-arrest.**

CHAPTER 13

THE ADMINISTRATION OF JUSTICE

IN THIS CHAPTER

- South Africa's Legal System
- General Questions
- Law of the Land True Story
- Takeaways

CHAPTER 13

THE ADMINISTRATION OF JUSTICE

South Africa's Legal System

The legal framework in South Africa has its roots in **Roman-Dutch law**, introduced during Dutch colonization in the 17th century. This system emphasized codified statutes and legal principles derived from Roman law. In the early 19th century, British colonization introduced **English common law** elements, particularly influencing procedural and commercial aspects of the legal system. Additionally, the 1996 Constitution formally acknowledged **customary law**, practiced by indigenous communities, as an integral part of the legal system, provided it aligns with constitutional principles and human rights .

The judiciary is organized into several tiers:[51]

- **Constitutional Court:** The highest court for constitutional matters, comprising 11 judges. It has the final authority on constitutional issues and ensures laws and government actions comply with the Constitution.
- **Supreme Court of Appeal:** Handles appeals from High Courts on non-constitutional matters and is based in Bloemfontein. It serves as the highest court for non-constitutional issues .

51 https://unimelb.libguides.com/c.php?g=929734&p=6718215

- **High Courts:** Divided into divisions across provinces, they handle serious civil and criminal cases and appeals from lower courts.
- **Magistrates' Courts:** Handle less serious civil and criminal cases at district and regional levels.
- **Specialist Courts:** Include the Labour Court, Land Claims Court, and others, focusing on specific legal areas.

South Africa's judiciary is notable for its commitment to upholding constitutional democracy and human rights. The Constitutional Court has played a pivotal role in shaping post-apartheid jurisprudence, ensuring that laws and government actions align with constitutional principles. Additionally, the formal recognition of customary law and traditional courts reflects the country's dedication to legal pluralism. However, despite its strengths, South Africa's judiciary faces **several persistent challenges**. One of the most pressing issues is a **shortage of judges** and the system's heavy reliance on acting judges, which has led to significant case backlogs and delays in justice delivery. Additionally, there have been reports of **bribery attempts and corruption** within the judicial system, which threaten to erode public trust in the rule of law. Furthermore, **access to justice remains uneven**, especially in rural and under-resourced communities, where limited infrastructure and legal services make it difficult for individuals to exercise their legal rights. Addressing these challenges is essential to preserving the integrity and functionality of South Africa's legal system.

General Questions

1. ***Will the court treat first-time offenders and tourists with more leniency?*** South African courts may consider first-time offender status and a person's background—such as being a tourist—when determining sentencing, but this does not guarantee leniency. Judges have discretion to weigh mitigating factors, including a clean criminal record, cooperation with authorities, expressions of remorse, and whether the offense was non-violent or due to ignorance of local laws. However, certain offenses—such as drug trafficking, sexual crimes, or violent acts—are treated with severity regardless of one's status as a foreigner or first-time offender. While tourists might receive more explanation or support in navigating the legal process, the law applies equally to citizens and foreigners. Legal representation is critical in such cases to argue mitigating circumstances effectively.

2. ***If I am charged with a crime, which court is likely to hear my case?*** If you are charged with a crime in South Africa, the court that hears your case depends primarily on the seriousness of the offense. Most criminal cases begin in the **Magistrates' Courts**, which are the lowest level of courts and handle the majority of criminal matters. Less serious offenses—such as theft, assault without severe injury, or traffic violations—are usually heard in the **District Magistrates' Court**. More serious charges—such as robbery, serious assault, or drug offenses—are handled in the **Regional Magistrates' Court**, which has broader sentencing powers. For the most serious crimes, such as murder, rape, or treason, the case may be escalated to the **High Court**, which also hears appeals from the lower courts.

3. ***What is the standard of proof in a criminal case in South Africa?*** In South Africa, the standard of proof in a criminal case is **"beyond a reasonable doubt."** This means the prosecution must present evidence strong enough to convince the court of the accused's guilt to the extent that there is no reasonable doubt in the mind of a reasonable person. It is a high standard designed to ensure that no individual is wrongfully convicted based on insufficient or uncertain evidence. If any reasonable doubt exists after considering all the evidence, the accused must be acquitted.

Law of the Land True Story[52]

The Mthatha High Court is at the center of a bribery scandal where court officials are accused of soliciting bribes for tasks they are already paid to perform. These tasks, which include retrieving "missing" case files, allocating court dates, transcribing orders, and expediting legal processes, have been reportedly held hostage for bribes as high as R15,000 (approximately $800 USD). Attorneys working with the court have confirmed the existence of this bribery ring, noting that well-resourced firms often pay bribes to ensure quick court dates, creating an uneven playing field for smaller firms and disadvantaged litigants.

Despite multiple complaints, including an anonymous letter sent to the court's leadership, no action has been taken. The corruption is said to have persisted for years, with some officials even allegedly demanding bribes in exchange for routine services like filing documents or securing court dates. This practice undermines the integrity of the judicial system, particularly affecting civil cases, which constitute a large portion of Mthatha's case load. The delay in taking action on the complaints highlights the systemic nature of the issue and the fear of retaliation among those who speak out.

52 https://www.dailymaverick.co.za/article/2025-05-05-mthatha-court-officials-ask-for-bribes-to-do-their-job/

Takeaways

- South Africa's legal system is a combination of Roman-Dutch law, English common law, and customary law, with the Constitutional Court serving as the highest authority on constitutional matters.
- Judicial challenges in South Africa include a shortage of judges, corruption, and delays in the justice system, as well as limited access to legal services in rural areas.
- First-time offenders and tourists may have their status considered by the court, but leniency is not guaranteed, especially for serious offenses like drug trafficking or violent crimes.
- Court structure for criminal cases depends on the severity of the offense, with less serious cases handled by Magistrates' Courts and more serious crimes escalated to higher courts, where the standard of proof is "beyond a reasonable doubt.

CHAPTER 14

CRIME VICTIM ASSISTANCE

IN THIS CHAPTER

- Overview
- What to Do If You Are the Victim of a Crime
- Common Tourist Scams in South Africa
- Consular Assistance
- General Questions
- Safety Tips

CHAPTER 14

CRIME VICTIM ASSISTANCE

Overview

In South Africa, the government has established a network of **Thuthuzela Care Centres** (**TCCs**) within selected public hospitals to provide an **integrated, one-stop response for victims of sexual violence**. Staffed by the National Prosecuting Authority, the South African Police Service, social workers and partner NGOs, these centers offer on-site medical examinations, crisis counseling, police investigation and support with court preparation, all designed to reduce secondary trauma and improve conviction rates.

Survivors of domestic and sexual violence can also access the **Gender-Based Violence National Command Centre** 24 hours for counseling, shelter referrals and legal information. For reporting any criminal activity anonymously, **Crime Stop** operates a tip-off line at **08600 10111**, and in emergencies victims can dial **10111** to reach the **South African Police Service** directly.

A range of non-governmental organizations complements these government efforts by offering specialized support services. The **Rape Crisis Cape Town Trust**, founded in 1976, operates 24-hour helplines in English (021 447 9762), isiXhosa (021 361 9085) and Afrikaans (021 633 9229), and provides free, confidential counseling, legal accompaniment and support groups.[53] **People Opposing Women Abuse** (POWA) offers free counslingfor victims of domestic and sexual abuse—along with children's services and legal referrals.[54] **Sonke Gender Justice** advocates to end gender-based violence and maintains several helplines, including the **Lifeline Sexual Health Line** and the **LoveLife Youth Line.**[55] For children affected by abuse, Childline South Africa provides a 24-hour counslingand legal advice service.[56]

What to Do If You Are the Victim of a Crime

If you become the victim of a crime, your first priority is your **personal safety** and that of anyone else with you. If you are in immediate danger, dial **10111** to summon the **South African Police Service** (**SAPS**). If the threat is less acute but you still feel unsafe, move to a secure location—perhaps a neighbor's home, a public building or any place you can lock—before placing the call.

Once you are safe, **preserve any evidence** of the offense. For violent crimes or sexual offences, avoid washing, changing clothes or disturbing the scene until after you have sought medical attention; doing so may compromise forensic evidence.

If you require medical care, go to the nearest public hospital or clinic and ask specifically to be referred to a **Thuthuzela Care Centre** (**TCC**) if the crime involves sexual violence—these centers offer free, integrated medical, counseling and forensic services under one roof.[57]

As soon as you are medically assessed, **report the incident** at the nearest police station. There, a police officer must open a case docket, take your statement and register you as a victim in terms of the Victims' Charter

53 https://rapecrisis.org.za/

54 http://www.powa.co.za

55 https://genderjustice.org.za/helpline-numbers/

56 https://childlinesa.org.za/

57 https://www.justice.gov.za/vg/sxo/2019-TCC-Brochure-Sep.pdf

(2015), which entitles you to be treated with dignity, respect and privacy, to receive information about the progress of your case, and to access protection and support services.[58] Remember to note the case or docket number and the name of the investigating officer.

After reporting, you can **request a copy of your statement** and ask the investigating officer how to obtain **updates.** You may also apply for a victim impact statement to be presented in court, detailing the emotional, physical and financial harm you've suffered; this can influence sentencing and entitle you to restitution or compensation. For monetary relief, enquire about the **Criminal Injuries Compensation Scheme** administered by the Department of Justice, which provides limited financial assistance to victims of violent crime.

Parallel to the criminal-justice process, it is vital to engage **support services** for counseling and legal advice. National helplines such as the **Gender-Based Violence National Command Centre** (0800 428 428 or "Please Call Me" to 1207867#) and NGOs like **POWA** (011 642 4345) or **Rape Crisis Cape Town Trust** (021 447 9762) offer free, confidential counseling, shelter referrals and legal accompaniment.

Finally, keep a **detailed personal diary** of all events related to your case—dates, times, names, conversations and any expenses incurred—as this will aid both your personal recovery and the legal process. Stay in regular contact with your Victim Liaison Officer at SAPS, attend all required court dates, and don't hesitate to seek further advice from **Legal Aid South Africa** if at any point you cannot afford private representation. By following these steps—prioritizing safety, preserving evidence, reporting promptly, accessing your rights under the Victims' Charter and engaging support services—you ensure that both your immediate needs and longer-term legal and emotional recovery are addressed.

58 https://www.justice.gov.za/VC/docs/vc/vc-eng.pdf

Common Tourist Scams in South Africa

Tourists in South Africa can fall prey to a variety of scams, ranging from the overtly aggressive to the seemingly benign. One of the most pervasive schemes involves informal **taxi or ride-hail services**. Scammers posing as legitimate drivers will flag you down, refuse to use the meter or demand cash upfront, then either overcharge you wildly or take you on a roundabout route to inflate the fare. In more brazen versions—particularly around airports—fraudsters **impersonate airport staff or "tourist police,"** insisting on handling your bags or guiding you to an ATM under the pretext of issuing a taxi voucher, then watching you enter your PIN before disappearing with your card. To avoid this, always book transfers through your hotel or a reputable app, insist on official badges, and refuse any unsolicited help with documentation or baggage (your driver should never need to see your boarding pass), particularly inside arrivals halls.[59]

ATM and credit-card scams are another significant hazard. Criminals often install skimming devices on machines and deploy accomplices to distract you—offering to "help" if your card is retained or pretending there's a technical fault—only to snatch your card or record your PIN. You may also encounter shrewd **pickpockets** who work in teams: one engages you in friendly conversation or stages a minor incident while another lifts valuables from your pocket or bag. Always use ATMs located inside bank branches or shopping centers, check for any loose parts or attachments on the keypad and card slot, cover your hand when entering your PIN, and never accept assistance from strangers at the machine

Street-level scams can be remarkably subtle. You might be approached by someone **offering a "free" friendship bracelet**, a sprig of rosemary for good luck, or a staged petition to support a charitable cause, only to find yourself pressured into paying once it's on your wrist or signed. Similarly, groups of **beggars**—sometimes feigning a sick child or disability—may ask you to accompany them to a nearby store, where they inflate the price of diapers or formula and split your payment. **Red flags**

59 https://www.hotels.com/go/south-africa/common-scams-cape-town?utm_source=chatgpt.com

include unsolicited gifts, insistence you follow them to a shop, or overly emotional stories designed to tug at your heartstrings. The safest response is a polite but firm refusal and, if you feel uneasy, to move on through a crowded area.

Accommodation and booking scams also target unwary travelers. **Fraudulent listings** on peer-to-peer platforms can advertise idyllic guesthouses or apartments that don't exist, or real properties that are already leased, only for you to discover at check-in that there is no reservation—and no refund. Equally common are **"timeshare" pitches** masquerading as "free" or deeply discounted tours: once you're in the room, you're subjected to high-pressure sales tactics and hidden fees. To steer clear of these, use well-established booking sites with secure payment systems, read multiple recent reviews, confirm cancellation policies in writing, and avoid any deal that demands large deposits before you've seen contracts or official property credentials.

Finally, **currency-exchange scams** can leave you short-changed. Street money-changers offering rates that undercut official bureaux can switch your bills for inferior denominations or counterfeit notes. They may also claim a "commission waiver" that vanishes once you've handed over your cash. Always exchange money at bank branches or licensed bureaus, count your bills discreetly before you leave the counter, and compare the rate on display with the central bank's published mid-market rate. If you suspect foul play, insist on a re-count in front of the teller or choose another vendor altogether.

By staying alert to these red flags—unmetered taxis, unsolicited "help," too-good-to-be-true deals, and street-corner exchanges—and by relying on reputable, official services, you can greatly reduce your risk of becoming a victim and focus instead on enjoying all that South Africa has to offer.

Consular Assistance

Consular assistance can be a vital lifeline if you fall victim to crime while traveling in South Africa, because your home-country diplomatic mission can help you navigate an unfamiliar legal system, explain your rights and even advocate on your behalf. For example, U.S. Consulates General in Johannesburg and Cape Town can advise you on how to report the offense to the South African Police Service, help you find reputable local medical and counseling services provide a list of English-speaking attorneys, and, with your written consent, notify your family or friends back home.[60] They can also assist with replacing a lost or stolen passport so you can continue your journey or return home, and in extreme cases offer an emergency loan for repatriation or limited financial support if you are destitute.[61]

Beyond practical support, consular officers act as a bridge between you and local authorities, helping to ensure that your case receives proper attention and that you understand each step of the criminal-justice process. They can request updates from the investigating officer, explain how to apply for compensation—such as through South Africa's Criminal Injuries Compensation Scheme—or guide you in preparing a victim impact statement. If you face language barriers, they can provide interpreters; if you fear intimidation, they can liaise with local officials to request your protection. By coordinating with NGOs and local victim-assistance programs, your consular post can help you access free counseling, shelter referrals and legal accompaniment, significantly reducing the stress of dealing with an overseas crime and allowing you to focus on recovery and your safe return home.

60 https://travel.state.gov/content/travel/en/international-travel/emergencies/crime .html

61 https://travel.state.gov/content/travel/en/international-travel/International-Travel-Country-Information-Pages/SouthAfrica.html

General Questions

1. ***If I am a victim of a crime, can I legally be compensated?*** **Yes.** You can be compensated for crime-related loss, damage or injury in South Africa through several legal routes. First, following a conviction you may ask the court to grant a **compensation order** under the Criminal Procedure Act (sections 297 & 300), which treats awarded sums as enforceable civil judgments. If there is no conviction or the perpetrator cannot pay, you can bring a **delictual (tort) claim** against the offender—or vicariously against the state—to recover damages for negligence by the South African Police Service. Additionally, victims can apply for limited financial relief via the Criminal Injuries Compensation Scheme administered by the Department of Justice.

2. ***If a family member falls victim to homicide, can I bring the body back to my home country?*** **Yes.** You may repatriate a family member's body from South Africa, but you must follow South African health and diplomatic procedures. First, the next of kin completes a sworn affidavit electing to return the mortal remains and submits it—together with the certified death certificate, post-mortem report, burial order from Home Affairs and an embalming certificate showing the body has been embalmed, sealed in an airtight container and placed in a sturdy coffin—to the Department of International Relations and Cooperation (DIRCO) via your nearest South African mission abroad. DIRCO will then liaise with the National Department of Health, which issues an import permit for non-infectious remains, and once all documentation is in place a South African–licensed funeral undertaker arranges the preparation, packaging and transport, ensuring that certified copies of the deceased's and next of kin's IDs or passports travel with the coffin.

3. ***Are there specific types of crimes that tourists in South Africa are more vulnerable to, and how can they reduce their risk?***
Yes. Tourists in South Africa are more vulnerable to certain types of crimes, particularly **petty theft, scams, muggings**, and **vehicle-related incidents** such as smash-and-grabs. These crimes often occur in busy urban centers, tourist areas, or isolated locations, especially where visitors may appear unfamiliar or distracted. To reduce their risk, tourists should avoid displaying valuables in public, use registered transport services, keep car windows up and doors locked, avoid walking alone at night, and stay informed about high-risk areas through local sources or hotel staff. Remaining aware of surroundings and taking common-sense precautions can significantly lower the likelihood of becoming a target.

Safety Tips

- Avoid displaying valuables like jewelry, phones, or cameras in public, especially in crowded or unfamiliar areas.
- Use registered taxis or ride-hailing apps instead of accepting rides from strangers or informal drivers.
- Stay alert at ATMs—only use machines inside banks or malls, cover your PIN, and never accept help from strangers.
- Keep car windows rolled up and doors locked, especially at traffic lights, to prevent smash-and-grab thefts.
- Don't walk alone at night or in isolated areas; travel in groups and stick to well-lit, busy streets.
- Be cautious of overly friendly strangers offering "free" gifts or emotional stories—these are often scams.

CHAPTER 15

POLICE

IN THIS CHAPTER

- Overview
- Police Response
- Police and Community Relations
- Police Use of Force
- Law of the Land True Story

CHAPTER 15

POLICE

Overview

The **South African Police Service** (**SAPS**) operates as a centralized, national police force under the direct control of the national government. Unlike federal systems such as those in the United States or Germany, South Africa **does not have separate state or municipal police departments** with independent authority. Instead, SAPS is governed by the Minister of Police and managed by a National Commissioner, who oversees policing across the entire country. While there are provincial commissioners and individual police stations in every region, these function as extensions of the national structure rather than autonomous bodies. Some major cities, such as Cape Town and Johannesburg, maintain municipal law enforcement units known as **Metro Police**. However, these units are limited in scope and primarily handle traffic enforcement, by-law compliance, and crime prevention. They are not authorized to conduct criminal investigations, which remain the responsibility of SAPS.

As of early 2024, SAPS has an estimated total staff of around 172,000 people, including approximately 140,000 sworn police officers and 32,000 civilian support personnel. With a national population of about 60 million, this equates to a police-to-citizen ratio of **roughly one officer for every 430 residents.**[62] While this might appear sufficient on

62 https://www.saps.gov.za/about/stratframework/annual_report/2022_2023/Annual-Report-2022-23-final-draft-2023-10-12.pdf

paper, SAPS is widely regarded as being **under-resourced and inadequately staffed** in practice. The number of personnel has declined, even as South Africa's population and crime rates have continued to rise. Many police stations, particularly in rural areas, struggle with staffing shortages, lack of vehicles, outdated infrastructure, and insufficient investigative support. Public concerns also include issues related to poor training, corruption, and low morale within the force. These factors have contributed to widespread criticism that SAPS is not equipped to effectively address the country's high levels of violent crime, organized criminal networks, and social unrest.

Police Response

The SAPS role is to prevent, investigate, and combat crime, uphold the law, maintain public order, and protect citizens and property. SAPS also supports emergency and disaster response and has specialized units such as the **Hawks** (Directorate for Priority Crime Investigation), which focus on organized crime, corruption, and terrorism (https://www.saps.gov.za/about/about.php).

The biggest challenges SAPS faces are deeply structural and wide-ranging. Violent crime remains extremely high—South Africa recorded over **27,000 murders** in the 2022/2023 reporting year, with the murder rate increasing by more than 50% since 2012 (https://www.saps.gov.za/services/crimestats.php). The police service is also burdened by significant **corruption**, including bribery, collusion with criminals, and misconduct in investigations. A 2023 report by Corruption Watch noted that the police sector was the **most reported institution for corruption** in South Africa (https://www.corruptionwatch.org.za/). The conviction rate for serious crimes remains underwhelming, partly due to poor investigative capacity and evidence handling.

Other operational challenges include **chronic understaffing** and **resource shortages**. The total number of SAPS employees has declined from over 193,000 in 2012 to around **172,000 in 2023**, including 140,000 sworn officers and 32,000 civilian staff, despite population growth and rising crime, with a current police-to-citizen of approximately

1:430, which well below optimal levels.[63] Rural and township areas are particularly affected by inadequate staffing, outdated vehicles, and slow response times.

To address these challenges, SAPS and the national government have introduced a range of reforms and strategic interventions. Since 2022, there has been a push to **recruit 10,000 new officers annually**, with a focus on improving visible policing and reducing violent crime in high-risk areas (https://businesstech.co.za/news/government/766825/south-africas-massive-police-problem/). The **Digital Case Docket System**, currently being piloted, aims to digitize and streamline criminal investigations and reduce case backlogs.

An important ongoing reform stems from the **2018 Panel of Experts Report on Policing and Crowd Management**, which called for the demilitarization of SAPS, improved training, and the responsible management of public protests. Implementation of these recommendations has been slow, but elements are reflected in the **National Policing Plan**, launched in 2023, which emphasizes **intelligence-led policing, better community engagement, and accountability mechanisms.**[64]

Finally, SAPS is investing in **Community Policing Forums (CPFs)** as part of a strategy to rebuild public trust and create a more community-centered approach to crime prevention. CPFs are meant to serve as a bridge between the police and residents, although their effectiveness varies significantly across the country due to inconsistent funding and support.[65] However, despite these reform efforts, many experts argue that without stronger oversight, better leadership, and deeper structural changes, the capacity of SAPS to manage South Africa's complex crime environment will remain limited.

---

63 https://www.defenceweb.co.za/security/civil-security/saps-cannot-keep-up-with-growing-population-one-police-officer-for-every-427-citizens/

64 https://www.policesecretariat.gov.za/downloads/reports/panel_of_experts_report_summary.pdf

65 https://issafrica.org/

Police and Community Relations

Public perception of the South African Police Service (SAPS) is widely negative, with low trust levels that have steadily declined in recent years. According to the **2023 Afrobarometer survey**, only **32% of South Africans** expressed any degree of trust in the police—just 11% said they trust SAPS "a lot," while 21% said "somewhat." In contrast, **43% of respondents** said they have **no trust at all** in the police, marking a significant deterioration from previous years.[66] A central reason for this lack of trust is the **widespread perception of police corruption and misconduct.** The same Afrobarometer report found that **61% of South Africans** believe that "most" or "all" police officers are involved in corruption, and **76%** believe that police officers engage in **illegal activities at least occasionally**, with 47% saying this happens "often" or "always".

Public dissatisfaction is also driven by **poor police service delivery.** A 2023 report based on the Governance, Public Safety and Justice Survey by Statistics South Africa noted that **almost 20% of people** reported the police **never responded** when called, while another 16% said **response times exceeded two hours.**[67]

Trust in police varies by region, with particularly low levels recorded in **Western Cape**, **Limpopo**, and **Gauteng.** In the Western Cape, for example, trust in SAPS dropped by over 20 percentage points between 2020 and 2021, significantly higher than the national drop of 7 points.[68]

These trust deficits have **serious implications for policing effectiveness**, especially in crime prevention and investigation. Lack of cooperation from the public due to fear or skepticism undermines crime reporting, witness cooperation, and broader community engagement. Efforts to address these issues include reforms aimed at improving

66 https://www.afrobarometer.org/publication/ad836-south-africans-view-of-police-marred-by-pervasive-corruption-lack-of-professionalism/

67 https://www.unodc.org/res/justice-and-prison-reform/access-to-justice-for-all_html/African_Policing_Civilian_Oversight_Forum.pdf

68 https://www.corruptionwatch.org.za/south-africans-have-low-trust-in-their-police-heres-why/

transparency, strengthening community policing forums, and enhancing the responsiveness and professionalism of SAPS officers. However, sustained change will depend on deeper institutional reform and long-term accountability.

Police Use of Force

Police use of force remains a **significant and persistent issue** in South Africa, with numerous recent cases highlighting concerns over excessive and sometimes lethal actions by law enforcement. The Independent Police Investigative Directorate (IPID) reported a notable increase in police misconduct for the 2023–2024 period. Specifically, there were **460 deaths due to police action**, marking a **17% increase** from the previous year. Additionally, 212 deaths occurred in police custody, and 273 cases of torture were reported, representing a 20% rise in such incidents. Alarmingly, there was also a **75% increase in reported cases of rape within police custody.**[69]

One particularly tragic recent incident involved the deaths of **87 miners** at the Buffelsfontein Gold Mine near Stilfontein. In an operation aimed at curbing illegal mining, authorities cut off food supplies to force the miners to surrender, leading to deaths from starvation or dehydration. This approach drew significant criticism from rights groups and prompted calls for an inquiry into the police's tactics.[70] (See *Law of the Land True Story* below.)

Public perception of the police is further marred by these incidents. According to a 2024 Afrobarometer survey, **76% of South Africans** believe that police officers engage in criminal activities at least occasionally, with **47%** asserting this occurs "often" or "always." Only about **24%** of

69 https://www.researchgate.net/publication/381437490_Examining_Violent_Police-Citizen_Encounters_in_South_Africa_A_Focus_on_Suspect_and_Police_Behaviour

70 https://apnews.com/article/south-africa-mine-miners-stilfontein-f5bd68beaee3e8c3babe801099ecee0e

citizens feel that the police operate in a professional manner and respect all citizens' rights.[71]

These statistics and incidents underscore the urgent need for comprehensive reforms within the South African Police Service to address misconduct and restore public trust.

Law of the Land True Story[72]

The tragic deaths of 87 miners at the Buffelsfontein Gold Mine in South Africa has brought renewed scrutiny to the South African Police Service (SAPS) and their use of force, particularly during operations targeting illegal mining. As reported by the Associated Press in January 2025, the miners, known locally as "zama zamas," perished underground after police cut off food and supply lines in a bid to force their surrender. This tactic, part of a broader anti-illegal mining crackdown dubbed "Operation Close the Hole," was intended to pressure miners to surface and face arrest. Instead, it led to starvation, dehydration, and death for dozens trapped deep underground.

Authorities denied responsibility, claiming the miners could have escaped through alternative shafts and that over 1,500 had already done so. However, civil rights groups argue that many miners were either too weak or too far from accessible exits to escape, and that dismantling the rope and pulley system used to supply the miners effectively sealed their fate. Delays in launching a rescue—only initiated after a court order—further fueled criticism.

The operation's harsh methods and the dismissive response from officials, including a cabinet minister who stated that "criminals are not to be helped," reflect deeper systemic issues in SAPS's handling

71 https://www.afrobarometer.org/publication/ad836-south-africans-view-of-police-marred-by-pervasive-corruption-lack-of-professionalism

72 https://apnews.com/article/south-africa-mine-miners-stilfontein-f5bd-68beaee3e8c3babe801099ecee0e

of vulnerable populations and use-of-force protocols. Critics contend that starvation was weaponized and question whether the miners' status as undocumented foreigners contributed to the extreme approach. The Democratic Alliance, South Africa's second-largest political party, has called for an official inquiry into whether SAPS is using punitive force as a standard response to crime, particularly when it intersects with migration and poverty.

CHAPTER 16

HOW TO GET LEGAL HELP IN SOUTH AFRICA

IN THIS CHAPTER

- Available Resources
- Legal Aid
- Foreign Embassies in South Africa

CHAPTER 16

HOW TO GET LEGAL HELP IN SOUTH AFRICA

Available Resources

If you are arrested in South Africa or require legal representation, there are several avenues for assistance. Foreign nationals who are arrested should immediately contact their country's embassy or consulate. These diplomatic missions can provide consular support and most of them maintain a list of local attorneys. For example, U.S. citizens can access lists of attorneys for specific cities through the U.S. Embassy in South Africa: for Cape Town at **https://za.usembassy.gov/attorneys-cape-town** and for Johannesburg at **https://za.usembassy.gov/attorneys-johannesburg.**

In addition to government resources, several independent organizations provide emergency legal assistance. **ProBono.Org** connects individuals with pro bono legal representation through partnerships with private law firms, and information on their services is available at **https://probono.org.za.** Lawyers for **Human Rights** (**LHR**) is another critical organization offering legal support to vulnerable individuals, including asylum seekers and undocumented migrants. Their legal help section can be accessed through the UNHCR portal at **https://help.unhcr.org/southafrica/get-help/legal.** Additionally, the **Southern Africa Litigation Centre** (**SALC**) focuses on human rights and constitutional litigation and works across the region to challenge unlawful arrests and abuses of power. Their work and contact information are detailed at **https://www.southernafricalitigationcentre.org**.

Many universities in South Africa also operate **legal clinics** that offer free or low-cost services, particularly in areas like family law, labor disputes, and access to social grants. One example is the University of KwaZulu-Natal's law clinics in Durban and Pietermaritzburg, which assist in a variety of social justice cases. For more information on these, consult university websites.

Legal Aid

Legal Aid in South Africa is primarily provided by **Legal Aid South Africa**, a state-funded public entity mandated to offer legal representation to those who cannot afford private legal services. It operates under the **Legal Aid South Africa Act (2014)** and functions independently from the courts and the police, ensuring its legal assistance is impartial and client focused.

Legal Aid covers both **criminal and civil matters**. In criminal cases, it provides representation to accused persons who face possible imprisonment and cannot afford a lawyer. In civil cases, Legal Aid assists with matters such as divorce, eviction, child custody, domestic violence, labor disputes, access to social grants, and housing rights. It also plays an advocacy role in promoting access to justice and constitutional rights.

To qualify for legal aid, applicants must meet **both a means test and a merit test**. The means test assesses income and assets: an individual must earn **less than R8,000 (about $425 USD)** per month after deductions and have assets valued below a certain threshold. Applicants with higher income or assets may still be considered in exceptional circumstances, particularly in complex or high-profile cases. The merit test ensures that the case has reasonable prospects of success or raises significant legal questions.

Foreign nationals, including visitors, are eligible for legal aid in certain circumstances. Legal Aid South Africa does not automatically exclude non-citizens; eligibility depends on the nature of the case and the individual's financial status. In criminal matters—especially where the accused is detained and faces imprisonment—foreigners are typically eligible, provided they meet the financial means test. In civil cases, Legal Aid may be more restrictive unless the matter involves human rights, children, or urgent humanitarian concerns.

The process for applying is straightforward. A person can apply by contacting any **Legal Aid South Africa Justice Centre**. During the application, individuals are required to provide identification (passport or other legal documents for foreigners), proof of income, and details about the legal issue. If detained, police or court officials may also facilitate contact with Legal Aid.

ADDITIONAL INFORMATION

Further information, including a list of Justice Centre locations, the means test calculator, and eligibility guidelines, is available on their official website at **https://legal-aid.co.za**.

Foreign Embassies in South Africa

Embassies and consulates are vital institutions that serve as the official representation of a country within a foreign nation. They play a crucial role in assisting travelers and expatriates by providing a range of services, including:

- **Emergency Assistance:** In cases of arrest, serious illness, or natural disasters, embassies can offer support and liaise with local authorities.
- **Document Services:** They issue or replace passports, notarize documents, and assist with visa applications.
- **Legal Support:** While embassies do not provide legal representation, they can offer information on local legal systems and provide lists of local attorneys.

- **Communication:** Embassies can help communicate with family members back home during emergencies.

Embassies and consulates in South Africa are predominantly concentrated in Pretoria, Cape Town, Johannesburg, and Durban. **Pretoria**, as the **administrative capital**, hosts the majority of foreign embassies and high commissions. **Cape Town**, being the **legislative capital**, accommodates numerous consulates-general, while **Johannesburg** and **Durban**, as major economic hubs, also have a significant diplomatic presence.

According to the University of Pretoria, there are approximately **196 foreign embassies and consulates in** South Africa. The Department of International Relations and Cooperation (DIRCO) provides a comprehensive directory of these foreign representations.[73] Countries with substantial diplomatic missions in South Africa include the United States, China, Germany, the United Kingdom, and India. The extensive presence of these nations is attributed to their significant economic, political, and historical ties with South Africa. For instance, the United States maintains an embassy in Pretoria and consulates in Cape Town, Johannesburg, and Durban, reflecting its broad engagement across various sectors.

U.S. Embassy Pretoria

877 Pretorius Street, Arcadia, Pretoria, 0083, South Africa
Phone: +27 (12) 431-4000
Email: protocolpretoria@state.gov
Website: https://za.usembassy.gov/u-s-embassy-pretoria/

U.S. Consulate General Johannesburg

1 Sandton Drive, Sandhurst, Johannesburg, 2196, South Africa
Phone: +27 (11) 290-3000
Fax: +27 (11) 884-0396
Email: consularjohannesburg@state.gov
Website: https://za.usembassy.gov/johannesburg-u-s-consulate/

73 https://www.up.ac.za/international-cooperation-division/article/2695512/foreign-embassies-and-consulates-in-south-africa

U.S. Consulate General Cape Town

2 Reddam Avenue, Westlake, Cape Town, 7945, South Africa
Phone: +27 (21) 702-7300
Fax: +27 (21) 702-7493
Email: americanscapetown@state.gov
Website: https://za.usembassy.gov/cape-town-u-s-consulate/

U.S. Consulate General Durban

303 Dr. Pixley KaSeme Street, 31st Floor, Delta Towers, Durban, 4001, South Africa
Phone: +27 (31) 305-7600
Fax: +27 (31) 305-7691
Email: consulardurban@state.gov
Website: https://za.usembassy.gov/durban-u-s-consulate/

CHAPTER 17

MEDICAL FACILITIES & HOSPITALS

IN THIS CHAPTER

- Overview
- Visitors' Access to Healthcare in South Africa
- South Africa's Hospitals
- Insurance Guidance
- General Questions

CHAPTER 17

MEDICAL FACILITIES & HOSPITALS

Overview

South Africa's healthcare system operates on a **dual-tier model**, comprising both public and private sectors. The **public healthcare system**, managed by the **Department of Health**, serves the majority of the population and is funded through taxation. It includes **over 400 public hospitals**, with large regional hospitals managed by provincial health departments and smaller hospitals and primary care clinics overseen by local municipalities . The **private sector**, on the other hand, is funded through private insurance and out-of-pocket payments, offering higher quality care with shorter wait times.[74]

In terms of accessibility, the public healthcare system aims to provide basic healthcare services to all citizens, including immigrants. However, it faces challenges such as resource limitations and longer waiting times. The private sector, while offering superior services, is accessible primarily to those who can afford private insurance or out-of-pocket expenses .

To address the disparities between the public and private sectors, the South African government has introduced the **National Health Insurance (NHI) Act** in 2023. This legislation aims to establish a national health insurance system to achieve universal access to quality

74 https://www.ibn.co.za/blog-and-news/q1-usa-healthcare

healthcare services, creating a single framework for public funding and purchasing of healthcare services.

For emergencies, South Africa has several important contact numbers:

- **10111:** Police emergency number
- **10177:** Ambulance and fire emergency services
- **112:** General emergency number accessible from any cellphone, connecting to a call center that routes to the appropriate emergency service

Visitors' Access to Healthcare in South Africa

While public healthcare is technically accessible to foreigners, it is less commonly used by visitors due to long wait times and perceived lower standards of care. Visitors to South Africa can access medical services through private healthcare facilities, which generally accept international travel insurance, direct out-of-pocket payments, or credit card payments. Many private healthcare providers require upfront payment or a deposit, even in emergencies, if the patient cannot immediately present valid insurance documentation or a payment guarantee, which can delay treatment. Not all South African medical facilities accept direct billing with foreign insurers, meaning visitors may need to pay upfront and then seek reimbursement, which can be bureaucratic and time-consuming. It's important to check whether the travel insurance provider has partner hospitals in South Africa or offers direct billing.

Out-of-pocket costs for private care vary depending on the service but are **relatively affordable by international standards**. A general consultation may cost between **$30 to $60 USD**, while emergency care and hospitalizations are significantly higher and often require a deposit upfront if insurance isn't accepted directly.[75]

75 https://www.internationalinsurance.com/health/systems/south-africa.php

Language barriers in South Africa are **generally minimal** in urban medical settings. English is one of the country's 11 official languages and is the primary language used in both public and private healthcare institutions, particularly in cities and tourist-heavy areas. Most doctors, nurses, and administrative staff speak fluent English, which means communication in medical contexts is rarely a problem for English-speaking visitors. However, in more rural areas, access to English-speaking professionals may be more limited.

Aside from payment and potential language issues, visitors to South Africa may face several challenges when seeking medical services. While major cities like Cape Town, Johannesburg, and Durban offer world-class private hospitals, **rural areas may lack well-equipped facilities and specialists.** Visitors in remote areas may need to be transported long distances for treatment, which can be costly and logistically challenging. In some regions with high crime rates or poor infrastructure, **emergency medical response can be delayed.** Private ambulance services are typically faster and more reliable but come at a higher cost.

Some medications commonly used abroad may not be available in South Africa or may go by different brand names. Visitors may also face **difficulties if their prescriptions** from home are not recognized or need to be reissued locally. It's recommended to carry an adequate supply of prescription medications along with documentation. Though rare, there have been reports of tourists being overcharged at some private facilities. Verifying prices in advance and using well-known hospital networks like **Mediclinic** or **Life Healthcare** can help mitigate this risk.

South Africa's Hospitals

South Africa's mixed public-private healthcare system includes approximately **420 public hospitals** and **about 215 private hospitals**, serving a population of over 60 million. The country also employs around 280,000 healthcare professionals, including doctors, nurses, and allied health workers, though distribution is uneven and urban-focused. Hospitals are primarily concentrated in major urban centers like Johannesburg, Cape Town, Pretoria, and Durban, where both public tertiary hospitals and private facilities are more accessible. Rural areas tend to have smaller clinics and limited access to specialists.

The quality of medical services varies significantly between the public and private sectors. South Africa's private healthcare is widely regarded as world-class, offering modern facilities, highly trained staff, and advanced medical technologies. Many doctors have international experience, and some hospitals are accredited by organizations like the Council for Health Service Accreditation of Southern Africa (COHSASA). (https://cohsasa.co.za/)

However, the public healthcare system faces challenges, including overcrowding, underfunding, and staff shortages, particularly in rural or high-demand areas.

Some of the best hospitals for international visitors include **Netcare Milpark Hospital** in Johannesburg, **Mediclinic Sandton**, and **Groote Schuur Hospital** in Cape Town. Private hospital groups such as **Netcare**, **Mediclinic**, and **Life Healthcare** operate many of the country's top facilities, known for excellent standards and English-speaking staff. These hospitals are popular with expats, tourists, and medical travelers seeking elective procedures.

Although there is no dedicated American hospital in South Africa, many private hospitals are internationally accredited or partner with global health organizations. For those seeking U.S.-linked care, Netcare's International Patients division provides assistance and coordination for foreign patients.

Insurance Guidance

As mentioned above, many private hospitals and clinics in South Africa accept foreign travel insurance, but **direct billing is not always guaranteed.** Travelers are often required to **pay upfront** and then seek reimbursement from their insurer later. However, some international insurers do have agreements with major hospital networks like Netcare and Mediclinic, so it's critical to verify in advance whether your provider offers direct billing or has local partners.

South Africa's private healthcare is significantly cheaper than in the U.S. As of 2024, estimated average prices in private hospitals are:

- **Emergency room visit:** $100–$300 depending on severity and services
- **General doctor consultation:** $40–$70
- **Specialist consultation:** $80–$150
- **Hospital admission (per night):** $150-550
- **Ambulance transport (private):** $100–$250
- **Basic lab tests or X-rays:** $20–$60
- **MRI or CT scan:** $250–$600

Prices vary by location and provider. More complex procedures and longer hospital stays increase costs significantly. When traveling to South Africa, it's strongly advised to purchase comprehensive travel insurance that includes emergency medical coverage, medical evacuation, trip cancellation, theft or loss of belongings, and coverage for activities like safaris or adventure sports. Reputable providers include **SafetyWing, World Nomads, Allianz, IMG**. Always read the policy details, buy coverage before your trip begins, and carry both digital and printed copies of your policy.

General Questions

1. ***What number do I call in a medical emergency in South Africa?*** In a medical emergency in South Africa, dial **112** from any mobile phone (free of charge) or **10177** from a landline. These numbers connect you to emergency medical services (EMS), including ambulances and paramedics.

2. ***Will I be treated if I don't have insurance?* Yes.** You will be treated without insurance, especially in life-threatening situations. Public hospitals are legally required to provide emergency care regardless of your ability to pay. However, the quality and speed of care in public facilities may be lower than in private hospitals.

3. ***Should I go to a public or private hospital?*** Travelers in South Africa should go to a **private hospital** if possible, as they offer better facilities, shorter wait times, and higher-quality care, however they are more expensive and usually require insurance or upfront payment.

4. ***What if I need a prescription in South Africa?*** If you need a prescription in South Africa, you can visit a local doctor or clinic to get one. Most pharmacies ("chemists") are well-stocked and widely available, including large chains like **Clicks** and **Dis-Chem.** Some medications available by prescription in the U.S. may be available over the counter in South Africa.

5. ***Can I bring my medication to South Africa?* Yes.** You can bring your medication to South Africa, but it's best to carry it in its original packaging along with a doctor's letter or prescription. Schedule 6 medications (strong narcotics or psychotropics) may require special permits, so check with the South African embassy before traveling if you're unsure.

6. ***What should I do in case of a medical emergency while traveling in South Africa?*** In case of a medical emergency in South Africa, dial **10177** for an ambulance or **112** for general emergencies, and provide clear details about your location. Contact your travel insurance provider for assistance and coverage details. Seek medical care at private hospitals like Netcare and Mediclinic **or** use private ambulance services like ER24 for quicker response times. Always carry a record of any medical conditions, allergies, medications, and your passport along with insurance information. Be prepared to pay upfront for care, as private healthcare can be costly.

CHAPTER 18

DRIVING IN SOUTH AFRICA

IN THIS CHAPTER

- Overview
- Main Traffic Rules & Road Safety Tips
- General Questions
- Law of the Land Hypothetical

CHAPTER 18

DRIVING IN SOUTH AFRICA

Overview

Driving in South Africa can be an enjoyable experience, especially for those seeking the freedom to explore diverse landscapes and remote areas. However, it comes with certain challenges that foreign drivers should be prepared for. Traffic in major cities like Johannesburg, Cape Town, and Durban can be heavy during peak hours, and aggressive driving is not uncommon. Outside urban areas, roads are generally less congested, but care should be taken on rural or poorly lit routes, especially at night. South Africans drive on the **left-hand side** of the road, and seat belts are mandatory for all passengers. Speed limits are strictly enforced, with cameras commonly used, and are typically 60 km/h (37 mph) in cities, 100 km/h (62 mph) on secondary roads, and 120 km/h (75 mph) on highways.

The **general condition of road infrastructure** varies. Major highways and primary routes are well maintained, particularly in and around cities and tourist corridors. However, rural roads can be in poor condition, with potholes, unmarked construction zones, or livestock crossings. In remote areas, 4x4 vehicles are often recommended. Street signage is in English and usually clear, although GPS or offline maps are highly advisable for navigation in more isolated regions.

Foreign drivers need a valid driver's license in English, or an **International Driving Permit (IDP)** if the original is not in English.

You must carry your passport, license, and proof of insurance while driving. Most rental cars include the minimum legally required insurance, but additional coverage for theft and collision is recommended.

There are a few **unique driving customs** to be aware of. On single-lane roads, it's customary to move onto the shoulder to allow faster drivers to pass, and drivers will often flash their hazard lights as a thank-you. Also, four-way stop signs are common in towns, and vehicles proceed in the order they arrived. Flashing headlights can indicate an oncoming hazard or a driver giving way. Be cautious at intersections and avoid driving at night in rural areas due to poor visibility and crime risk.

Toll roads are common on national highways such as the N1, N3, and N4. Toll fees vary by route and vehicle type, ranging from about **$1 to $10 USD.** Payment can usually be made with cash (South African rand), credit cards, or an electronic tag (like the **e-tag** used in rental cars). Check with your rental agency if your car is equipped with one, as this can allow quicker passage through dedicated lanes.

Main Traffic Rules & Road Safety Tips

- **Driving side:** South Africans drive on the left-hand side of the road, with the steering wheel on the right side of the vehicle.
- **Speed limits:**
  - **Urban areas:** 60 km/h (37 mph)
  - **Secondary/open roads:** 100 km/h (62 mph)
  - **National highways/freeways:** 120 km/h (75 mph) Speed limits are strictly enforced by fixed and mobile cameras.
- **Traffic signals:** Standard international traffic lights (red, yellow, green) are used. Four-way stop signs are common, and vehicles proceed in the order of arrival. Treat out-of-order traffic lights with

extreme caution—especially in cities where power outages ("load shedding") are common.

- **Seat belts:** Seat belts are mandatory for all passengers. Children under the age of 3 must be in a car seat, while those between 3 and 14 must use a child restraint or seat belt if available.
- **Alcohol:** The legal blood alcohol limit is 0.05% and 0.02% for professional drivers. South African police conduct roadside breath tests, and penalties for DUI include heavy fines, license suspension, and possible jail time.
- **Mobile devices:** Using a hand-held phone while driving is illegal. Only hands-free devices are permitted.
- **If stopped by police:** Always remain calm and respectful. You may be asked to show your passport, driver's license, and proof of vehicle insurance. Do not offer bribes, as bribery is illegal and may be prosecuted. If you feel uncomfortable, ask to be escorted to the nearest police station.
- **Road safety:** South Africa has a relatively high road accident rate. Drive defensively, stay alert, and take extra care on rural roads or when weather conditions are poor. Consider renting a well-maintained vehicle, ideally with roadside assistance included. Always keep windows rolled up and doors locked in urban areas. Watch for pedestrians, cyclists, and livestock, especially outside cities. Refuel often, as gas stations can be far apart in remote areas.

General Questions

1. ***What is the age requirement for renting a car in South Africa?*** The minimum age to rent a car in South Africa is typically **18 to 23 years**, depending on the rental company. Most major rental agencies require drivers to be at least **21 years old**, and they usually charge a **young driver surcharge** for anyone under **25.**

2. ***What is the availability of roadside assistance for foreign drivers in South Africa?*** Roadside assistance is widely available for foreign drivers in South Africa, and it's recommended to include this service in your rental agreement. Many car rental companies offer roadside assistance, covering services like flat tire changes, fuel delivery, and emergency towing. It's advisable to confirm the specifics with your rental agency before your trip. Organizations like the **Automobile Association (AA)**, **Nissan Assistance**, and **Opel Assistance** provide roadside services, including 24/7 support. You can also contact emergency services like ambulance (10177), police (10111), and fire services (10111) in case of urgent situations.

3. ***What are the parking regulations for foreign drivers in South Africa, and are there any areas where parking is restricted or unsafe?*** In South Africa, parking regulations are relatively straightforward, but foreign drivers should be aware of certain rules. Pay parking areas are common in urban centers like Cape Town and Johannesburg, especially in commercial districts, and fees can be paid at parking meters or via mobile apps such as **ParkNow** or **SnapScan**. It's important to always check for **no parking** signs or areas marked for specific purposes, like loading zones or reserved parking. Unauthorized parking can result in fines or towing. Many shopping malls, hotels, and residential areas offer **private parking**, but some may be gated or require access passes, so be sure to confirm that parking is allowed. Avoid parking in unfamiliar or high-crime areas, particularly at night, and never leave valuables in plain sight. In some cities like Johannesburg, Cape Town, and Durban, security concerns may

restrict parking in certain locations. If you receive a parking ticket, be sure to pay it within the required time to avoid additional fines, and in case your vehicle is towed, contact the local municipal traffic department to retrieve it.

Law of the Land Hypothetical

HYPOTHETICAL: *Emma, a tourist from the UK, is driving along a rural highway from Cape Town to the Garden Route. She's unsure of the speed limit and is driving at what she thinks is a safe speed. A police officer pulls her over and informs her she was speeding at 80 km/h in a 60 km/h zone. Emma believes the signage was unclear, and the officer asks for her passport, international driver's permit (IDP), and rental car documents. After reviewing them, the officer issues a speeding fine and requests immediate payment. What should Emma do in this situation, and how should she handle the speeding fine?*

ANSWER: *Emma should stay calm and respectful. If a speeding fine is issued, she must pay it within the required time, even if she disagrees with the officer's assessment. She can ask the officer for clarification on the speed limit signs but should accept the fine. She can pay immediately if she has cash or a card or ask for alternative payment methods. If she wishes to contest the fine, she can take legal action in court, though this may delay her plans. To avoid future issues, Emma should familiarize herself with local road signs and ensure her rental car has all necessary documentation.*

CHAPTER 19

NUDE BEACHES & CLOTHING-OPTIONAL RESORTS

IN THIS CHAPTER

- Overview
- Legality and Safety
- General Questions
- Law of the Land Hypothetical

CHAPTER 19

NUDE BEACHES & CLOTHING-OPTIONAL RESORTS

Overview

In South Africa, nudism is **not widely practiced or culturally mainstream**, but there are specific areas where it is **accepted and practiced.** The country has a small but active nudist community, and there are designated areas, particularly beaches and resorts, where nudism is allowed.

The most famous nude beach in South Africa is **Sandy Bay** near Cape Town. This secluded beach is well-known for its relaxed, clothing-optional atmosphere. **Llandudno Beach** in Cape Town and **De Hoop Nature Reserve** also have unofficial nudist-friendly areas, although they may not be explicitly designated.

There are also **nudist resorts** and **private accommodations** that cater specifically to nudists. **The Naked Garden** near Stellenbosch and **Cango Retreat** in Oudtshoorn are examples of places where nudism is welcomed, providing a safe, non-judgmental environment for those wishing to embrace this lifestyle.

However, outside of these specific locations, public nudity is generally **not acceptable** in South Africa, and **local laws** prohibit nudity in public spaces. It's important for visitors to respect cultural norms and legal regulations, especially in urban areas and public places.

Legality and Safety

In South Africa, **local decency laws** play a significant role in regulating nudism. These laws govern public behavior and maintain public order, including prohibiting **nudity in public spaces** outside designated areas. The **Criminal Law (Sexual Offenses and Related Matters) Amendment Act** outlines provisions for **public indecency**, which includes nudity in areas where it is not explicitly allowed, such as streets, parks, or urban settings. Public indecency charges can be brought against individuals who are caught naked in public outside of a legally recognized nudist area, such as a designated **nudist beach** or **private nudist resort**.

While **nudism** is **not illegal in private spaces**, it's crucial to respect local laws that specify where nudity is permitted. This means that public nudity outside designated areas, like **Sandy Bay** or **Llandudno Beach**, which are known for their acceptance of nudism, can lead to legal repercussions. In addition, while there is some tolerance in these specific areas, it is still important to **adhere to local norms** and always be aware of the laws in place for public conduct.

Nudist etiquette in South Africa mirrors global practices and centers around **respect for others' privacy and consent**. Visitors to nudist beaches or resorts should always be mindful of **personal space** and avoid actions that could make others uncomfortable. **Photographs** should only be taken with explicit consent, and one should **never engage in sexual activities** in public or nudist spaces, as this can lead to legal issues and a disruptive environment. Visitors should also cover up when leaving designated nudist areas, as wearing clothing in non-designated areas is both **socially expected** and legally required.

Before visiting any nudist-friendly location, it's always a good idea to **familiarize yourself** with the **specific rules and guidelines** of the venue or beach to ensure you are following proper etiquette. These might include guidelines about behavior, noise levels, and restrictions on alcohol or other activities. Always ensure that the establishment you are visiting is legally recognized for nudism and remain respectful of the surrounding community and legal boundaries. By understanding local decency laws and practicing good etiquette, you can enjoy a positive and legally safe experience in South Africa's nudist spaces.

As always, safety should be a priority, and you should consider the following factors:

- **Research the Destination:** Look for established nudist beaches or resorts with good reviews. Online forums and social media can provide insights from fellow travelers about safety and experiences.
- **Local Regulations:** Familiarize yourself with the rules of the specific beach or resort. Some places may have designated areas for nudism, while others might be more lenient. Adhering to local customs helps ensure a positive experience.
- **Travel in Groups:** If possible, visit with friends or fellow travelers. There's safety in numbers, and it can enhance the experience to share it with others.
- **Stay Aware of Your Surroundings:** As with any beach or resort, it's wise to be aware of your environment. Keep personal belongings secure and be cautious of anyone acting suspiciously.
- **Trust Your Instincts:** If a place feels uncomfortable or unwelcoming, it's okay to leave and seek another location.
- **Respect Others' Privacy:** Nudist communities value consent and privacy. Always be respectful of others and avoid taking photos without permission.

General Questions

1. ***What are the potential legal consequences for public nudity outside designated nudist areas in South Africa?*** In South Africa, public nudity outside designated nudist areas can result in legal consequences under public decency laws. Public nudity in non-designated spaces like streets or parks is considered public indecency, and offenders may face **fines, arrest, or imprisonment.**

2. ***What are the main health and safety considerations for visitors practicing nudism at South African beaches or resorts?*** When practicing nudism at South African beaches or resorts, sun protection is essential, so be sure to use high-SPF sunscreen, wear a hat, and stay hydrated. Hygiene is important, so use designated facilities for changing and showering, and bring personal hygiene items like towels. Be mindful of potential marine hazards like jellyfish or sea urchins and stay alert to safety warnings. Additionally, protect your belongings from theft by securing valuables in a safe area, as theft can be an issue at some locations.

3. ***Are there any age restrictions or family-friendly guidelines for visitors to nudist beaches or resorts in South Africa?*** In South Africa, nudist beaches and resorts are generally family-friendly, with age restrictions typically not enforced. For instance, Sun Eden Naturist Resort in Pretoria welcomes children of all ages, emphasizing a family-oriented environment. However, it's important to note that some nudist resorts may have specific guidelines to ensure a comfortable experience for all guests. For example, Sun Eden Naturist Resort prohibits overt sexual activity and the use of cameras or cell phones with photo capabilities to maintain a respectful atmosphere.
   While nudist beaches like Sandy Bay in Cape Town and Mpenjati Beach in KwaZulu-Natal are popular among naturists, they may not have formal age restrictions. It's advisable for families to visit during daylight hours and to exercise discretion when choosing a location. **To ensure a positive experience, it's recommended to**

research specific venues beforehand, adhere to posted rules, and maintain respectful behavior towards other guests.

Law of the Land Hypothetical

HYPOTHETICAL: *Sarah, a tourist in South Africa, is visiting Cape Town and decides to spend the day at Sandy Bay, a popular beach known for its unofficial acceptance of nudism. While enjoying the beach, Sarah notices another group of tourists setting up camp in a secluded area, and they are engaging in inappropriate behavior, including taking explicit photos of others without permission. Sarah feels uncomfortable and wonders whether this is legal, especially considering she is unaware of specific rules for nudist areas in South Africa.*

ANSWER: *In South Africa, taking explicit photos of others without their consent is a violation of privacy rights under the Protection of Personal Information Act (POPIA). Especially at nudist beaches, individuals must respect others' privacy, and unauthorized photography is prohibited. If Sarah feels uncomfortable, she can approach the beach's security or contact local authorities to report the behavior. It's essential to remember that all photos in public spaces must be taken with permission, and Sarah should familiarize herself with any specific rules at the venue.*

CHAPTER 20

UNUSUAL LAWS

IN THIS CHAPTER

- Overview
- South Africa's Unusual Laws and Associated Penalties
- General Questions
- Law of the Land Hypothetical

CHAPTER 20

UNUSUAL LAWS

Overview

Unusual laws can be fascinating glimpses into a culture's values and history. While most people are aware of common legal restrictions, it's often the strange and quirky laws that capture our attention. These regulations can range from the amusing to the absurd, reflecting the unique circumstances and traditions of a place. Whether they arise from historical events, societal norms, or simply peculiar local customs, unusual laws can provide insight into the quirks of human behavior and governance.

HELPFUL TIPS

South Africa's Unusual Laws and Associated Penalties

South Africa has its share of unique laws that may surprise visitors. While many are rooted in public safety, cultural norms, or environmental concerns, they can catch foreigners off guard if they're unaware. Here are a few of such quirky laws:

Driving barefoot is illegal:

It is technically illegal to drive barefoot in South Africa. While this law is rarely enforced, it's considered a safety risk because it may reduce the control a driver has over the pedals, especially in an emergency. Penalty: A fine or penalty for not adhering to traffic safety regulations.

It's illegal to "feed" pigeons in some public areas

In cities like Cape Town and Johannesburg, it's illegal to feed pigeons in public spaces. The law aims to prevent the spread of disease and keep public areas clean. Penalty: A fine for feeding pigeons in restricted public areas.

No flipping the bird (middle finger) in public

In South Africa, using obscene gestures such as flipping the middle finger at someone can be considered a criminal offense. It can be charged under the Public Indecency Act, which prohibits offensive behavior in public. Penalty: Fines or even imprisonment for public indecency.

It's illegal to use a toy gun in public

South African law requires that toy guns, including those that look realistic, must be clearly marked to avoid confusion with real weapons. Using a toy gun in public spaces can cause unnecessary panic or be mistaken for a real weapon. Penalty: Fines or the possibility of the toy gun being confiscated.

You can't keep a crocodile as a pet

In South Africa, it is illegal to keep a crocodile as a pet, as it is considered dangerous and a threat to public safety. The law restricts the ownership of certain exotic animals unless you have a special permit for them. Penalty: Fines or the confiscation of the animal, and in some cases, a prison sentence for illegal animal ownership.

General Questions

1. ***Can I get into legal trouble for swearing at someone in public in South Africa?*** Yes. Swearing, especially at officials or in public, can be prosecuted under crimen injuria, which protects personal dignity.

2. ***Is it legal to ride in the back of a pickup truck (bakkie) in South Africa?*** Only if you're not paying for the ride. Carrying passengers in the back for commercial transport is illegal and can lead to fines.

3. ***Can I honk my car horn anywhere in South Africa?*** No. Hooting is restricted near hospitals, schools, and places of worship. Violations may result in spot fines under local bylaws.

Law of the Land Hypothetical

HYPOTHETICAL: *Nina, a traveler from Brazil, wants to buy a bottle of wine to enjoy with dinner on Good Friday while staying in a coastal town in South Africa. When she tries to purchase it at a local liquor store, she's told alcohol sales are prohibited that day. Confused, she asks whether this is a store policy or a national rule. Is it illegal to buy alcohol on Good Friday in South Africa?*

ANSWER: *Yes. South African law prohibits the sale of alcohol on certain religious public holidays, including Good Friday, unless the establishment holds a special license (like a restaurant or hotel with on-site consumption rights). Violating this restriction can result in fines or license suspension for retailers. Visitors should plan ahead if they want alcohol during those times.*

CHAPTER 21

TRAVELING SAFELY

IN THIS CHAPTER

- Ladies Traveling Solo
- Traveling as a Family
- Advice for All Travelers
- Do's and Don'ts While in South Africa

CHAPTER 21
TRAVELING SAFELY

Ladies Traveling Solo

While some solo female travelers have positive experiences in South Africa, the country is **largely regarded as unsafe for solo travel**—especially for women—by most international safety indexes and travel advisories. South Africa has high rates of violent crime, including gender-based violence, and this shapes both its local and global safety reputation. Petty crime, theft, and more serious incidents like assault can occur, particularly in urban areas and after dark. The U.S. State Department currently ranks South Africa at **Level 2: Exercise Increased Caution**, but it specifically highlights risks to women, especially at night and in isolated areas. Local and foreign women alike are urged to take strong safety precautions and avoid traveling alone in unfamiliar areas.

That said, it's not unmanageable. Many women do travel solo there, but they tend to stick to safer, tourist-oriented regions (like the Garden Route, Cape Town's Atlantic Seaboard, or guided safaris) and rely on secure transport and accommodations. The key is understanding the risks, preparing thoroughly, and avoiding high-risk areas like inner-city Johannesburg, certain parts of Durban, and walking alone after dark anywhere.

South Africa offers incredible experiences for solo female travelers, but it's important to prioritize safety to ensure a positive trip. Here are some essential safety tips tailored specifically for solo female travelers in South Africa:

- **Research your destination thoroughly:** Check current travel advisories and local news before visiting any area. Talk to the hotel or resort personnel or a trusted local what areas to avoid.
- **Stick to well-populated areas:** Avoid venturing into isolated areas, especially at night.
- **Use licensed taxis and ride-sharing services:** Be cautious about using street taxis and always confirm the route with the driver.
- **Inform someone of your plans:** Let a trusted friend or family member know your itinerary and expected return times.
- **Be aware of your surroundings:** Stay vigilant and trust your instincts.
- **Dress modestly in certain areas:** Depending on the region, dressing conservatively can help you avoid unwanted attention.
- **Have local emergency numbers saved on your phone:** In South Africa, dial **10111** for police and **112** for general emergencies. Also, familiarize yourself with the nearest embassy or consulate in case you need assistance.

Traveling as a Family

Traveling with children in South Africa can be a rewarding and educational experience, but it requires careful planning to ensure their safety and health throughout the trip. One of the first steps is addressing **health precautions.**

Make sure your children are up to date on **routine vaccinations** and consider additional ones such as hepatitis A, typhoid, or malaria prophylaxis if you're visiting areas like Kruger National Park where the risk is higher. Protect against mosquito bites by using child-safe insect repellent, dressing children in long sleeves and pants in the evenings, and using mosquito nets where appropriate. **Sun protection** is also critical due to South Africa's high UV index—apply a high SPF sunscreen regularly, and ensure your children wear hats and protective clothing during peak sunlight hours. Stick to **bottled or purified water,** particularly in rural areas, to avoid gastrointestinal issues.

Safety is another major consideration. Always book accommodations that are **secure** and **family-friendly,** ideally with childproofed rooms and enclosed outdoor areas. **Avoid high-crime areas**, particularly at night, and stick to well-trafficked tourist routes. When traveling by car, ensure that children are properly restrained in **car seats** and that vehicles are roadworthy. South Africa has well-maintained roads in tourist regions, but conditions can vary significantly in rural zones, so drive cautiously. Educate your children about **basic safety rules** such as staying close to adults in public areas and not talking to strangers.

Comprehensive travel insurance is essential. Make sure it covers emergency medical treatment, hospital stays, and potential evacuation. Also confirm that it includes coverage for safari-related incidents if you plan to visit wildlife parks. On safari, only go with reputable guides who offer child-friendly tours and always follow all safety instructions. Children should not be left unattended in game areas, and many safari lodges have age restrictions, so check in advance.

Food safety is another concern. Choose restaurants with strong hygiene standards and avoid street food or anything that looks undercooked or has been sitting out. If your child has food allergies, inform the staff clearly and carry allergy cards if needed. Supervise what your child eats and drinks, and pack familiar snacks for situations where options are limited.

Swimming and outdoor activities require vigilance. South Africa has many beautiful beaches, but currents can be dangerous and not all beaches have lifeguards. Always supervise children near water and teach them about water safety. Whether it's a beach, a pool, or a river, never assume safety without checking the conditions first.

Finally, always **be prepared for emergencies**. Save local emergency numbers to your phone—**10111** for **police** and **112 for general emergencies**—and consider purchasing a local SIM card for reliable service.

Carry a well-stocked **first aid kit**, including any necessary medications, antiseptics, and insect repellent. Staying connected and prepared ensures you can act quickly if any issues arise.

Advice for All Travelers

South Africa is a beautiful and diverse country that attracts millions of visitors each year, however it's also a country where travelers need to stay alert and take precautions to ensure a safe and smooth trip. Understanding potential risks ahead of time can help you avoid trouble and focus on enjoying your experience.

Crime is the most significant concern for most travelers. While millions visit without incident, South Africa has high rates of petty and violent crime in certain areas. Tourists are particularly vulnerable to pickpocketing, bag snatching, and scams in busy urban centers like Johannesburg, Durban, and Cape Town. To reduce your risk, avoid displaying valuables such as smartphones, jewelry, or expensive cameras in public, especially in crowded markets or transport hubs. Don't leave bags or personal items unattended, even in restaurants or vehicles. Always keep your passport, money, and important documents in a secure place, preferably in a money belt or a hotel safe.

Another concern is **car-related crime**. Smash-and-grab thefts from vehicles are common, especially when stopped at intersections or traffic lights. Keep windows rolled up, doors locked, and valuables out of sight at all times while driving. Avoid driving after dark in unfamiliar or poorly lit areas, particularly in rural regions where emergency assistance can be limited. Carjackings and roadside scams also occur, so be cautious if flagged down unexpectedly—only stop for clearly marked police or security vehicles, and when in doubt, drive to the nearest police station or public area.

ATM and credit card fraud is a known issue. Use ATMs inside shopping malls, banks, or other secure locations rather than on the street. Shield your PIN and avoid accepting help from strangers while using the machine. Regularly check your bank account for unauthorized charges and notify your bank of your travel plans to avoid complications.

In terms of health and hygiene, be mindful of water safety and food preparation standards, especially in rural or less-developed areas. Tap water is safe to drink in most major cities, but bottled water is recommended in outlying regions. Stick to well-reviewed restaurants and avoid undercooked or street food unless you're confident of its hygiene.

Another general consideration is **local awareness.** While South Africa is diverse and relatively open, cultural norms can vary significantly between urban and rural areas. In conservative communities, dress modestly and be respectful of local customs. Avoid discussing sensitive topics like politics, race relations, or crime with strangers, as these can be polarizing.

Finally, **always stay informed about your surroundings.** Monitor local news and weather reports and register with your embassy or consulate upon arrival. Protests, power outages (load shedding), or local unrest can disrupt travel plans, and being informed helps you respond quickly and appropriately.

Do's and Don'ts While in South Africa

When visiting South Africa, understanding the country's cultural and social norms can go a long way in ensuring respectful, meaningful interactions. South Africa is known as the "Rainbow Nation" for its cultural and ethnic diversity, so etiquette can vary by region, community, and context. Still, there are some broadly accepted do's and don'ts that travelers should keep in mind.

DO'S:

- **Greet People Politely:** South Africans generally appreciate friendly and respectful greetings. A handshake, often accompanied by direct eye contact and a smile, is common—though in some communities, especially among older or more traditional people, a slight bow or nod might be more appropriate. Always greet elders and people in positions of authority with respect.

- **Be Open and Respectful of Diversity:** South Africa has 11 official languages and a mix of cultures including Zulu, Xhosa, Afrikaans, English, Indian, and others. Show interest in learning about local customs, languages, or traditions. Asking respectful questions is often welcomed.
- **Use Titles and Formal Address When Appropriate:** When meeting someone for the first time or in a formal setting, use "Mr.," "Mrs.," or a professional title. First-name use may follow, but wait to be invited.
- **Ask Before Taking Photos:** Always ask permission before photographing people, especially in rural or traditional communities. Some may feel uncomfortable being photographed, and others may expect a small tip.
- **Be Punctual in Professional Settings:** In business or formal environments, punctuality is important and appreciated. In casual social settings, being a little late is generally more acceptable.
- **Use Both Hands When Giving or Receiving Something:** It's considered polite to use both hands or the right hand supported by the left when handing something to someone, especially elders or in rural areas.

DON'TS:

- **Don't Assume Everyone Shares the Same Culture or Beliefs:** South Africa is extremely diverse, so avoid generalizing or making assumptions about people based on appearance, language, or accent. What's acceptable in one community may not be in another.
- **Don't Make Jokes About Race or Apartheid:** Race relations and the legacy of apartheid are still deeply felt and politically sensitive.

Avoid making jokes, comments, or assumptions about these topics, especially with people you've just met.

- **Don't Engage in Public Displays of Wealth:** Wearing flashy jewelry or showing expensive belongings can be seen as insensitive in a country with significant poverty and may also make you a target for theft.
- **Don't Point with Your Finger:** Pointing directly at people can be considered rude in some South African cultures. Instead, gesture with your whole hand or nod in the direction you're referring to.
- **Don't Enter Someone's Home Without Being Invited:** Always wait to be invited into someone's home and follow the host's cues once inside. In many traditional households, there may be specific areas or customs to observe.
- **Don't Be Disrespectful of Wildlife or Natural Sites:** Many South Africans hold their natural environment in high regard. Respect national parks, don't litter, and follow all rules during safaris or nature excursions.

CHAPTER 22

TOURIST TAXATION

IN THIS CHAPTER

- Overview
- Tourist Taxes in South Africa
- Law of the Land Hypothetical

CHAPTER 22
TOURIST TAXATION

Overview

Tourism plays a significant role in South Africa's economy, contributing substantially to both the GDP and employment. As of 2024, the tourism sector accounted for approximately **7% of South Africa's GDP** and supported over **1.7 jobs**, with indirect benefits reaching sectors like retail, transport, and hospitality.[76] The country's rich natural landscapes, wildlife, and cultural heritage attract millions of visitors annually, making tourism a key driver of foreign exchange and local development.

Tourists are required to pay certain taxes in South Africa, such as **Value-Added Tax** (**VAT**) and **bed tax**, which are they're common worldwide and designed to ensure that visitors contribute to the infrastructure and services they use during their stay. The revenue from tourist taxes helps fund essential public services and maintain infrastructure that benefits both locals and visitors. Funds collected through VAT and tourism taxes support the upkeep of national parks, public transport, road networks, water systems, and safety services. Additionally, part of this revenue is often reinvested into tourism development and marketing initiatives, particularly in rural or emerging destinations that depend heavily on tourism for local income.

76 ca.net/gl/en/corporate/page/south-african-tourism-annual-report

Tourist Taxes in South Africa

Tourists visiting South Africa are subject to a few key taxes that help support the country's infrastructure, tourism promotion, and public services. These taxes are typically included in the cost of goods and services, and in most cases, visitors don't need to take additional steps to pay them.

The most common tax is the **Value Added Tax** (**VAT**), which is a **15% consumption tax** included in the price of most goods and services. Tourists automatically pay VAT on purchases like meals, hotel stays, tours, and shopping. However, visitors can claim a **VAT refund** on goods they take out of the country, as long as the total value exceeds **R250** (**about $13 USD**). To qualify, tourists must present original tax invoices with the seller's information, VAT amount, and item descriptions. Refunds can be processed at **VAT Refund Administrator** offices located in major airports, border posts, and harbors before departure.[77]

Another tax that applies to many tourists is the **Tourism Levy** (**TOMSA**), a **1% fee** on certain travel-related services such as **hotel accommodations, tour operators,** and **car rentals**. Although it's technically a voluntary levy paid by businesses, it's passed on to travelers at participating establishments and automatically added to their bills. This levy helps promote South Africa as a tourist destination and supports industry initiatives.[78]

Lastly, there's an **Air Passenger Tax** on international flights departing from South Africa. This tax is **R100** (**about $5 USD**) for flights to nearby countries like Botswana, Lesotho, Namibia, and Eswatini, and **R190** (**about $10 USD**) for flights to other international destinations. This tax is included in the cost of the airline ticket, so travelers don't need to pay it separately.

Tourists visiting South Africa should be aware of a few additional points regarding taxation. First, while VAT refunds are available, they apply

77 https://www.globalvatcompliance.com/vat-rates-in-south-africa

78 https://tbcsa.travel/tomsa/

only to physical goods—such as clothing, electronics, or souvenirs—that are taken out of the country. Services like hotel stays, meals, or tours are not eligible for a refund. To successfully claim a VAT refund, travelers must request and keep **original tax invoices** that include the seller's name, VAT registration number, the amount of VAT paid, and a clear description of the goods purchased. Not all receipts qualify, so it's important to ask for a proper tax invoice at the time of purchase.

VAT refund claims must be processed **before leaving South Africa**, typically at designated VAT Refund Administrator offices located at international airports, land border posts, or harbors. **Once you've exited the country, claims can no longer be submitted.** For most tourists, there are no issues with double taxation, as South Africa does not tax foreign income unless you stay more than 183 days in a year and earn income from a South African source. Refunds and pricing are generally issued in South African rand, and currency conversion fees or administrative charges may slightly reduce the final refund amount. Additionally, most reputable tour operators and accommodations are transparent about VAT and the 1% tourism levy, indicating whether these are included in the advertised price or added at checkout. Understanding these rules allows travelers to avoid surprises and take advantage of available savings while contributing fairly to the local economy.

Law of the Land Hypothetical

HYPOTHETICAL: *Emily, a tourist from Canada, visits South Africa for two weeks. During her trip, she buys a handcrafted leather jacket from a boutique in Cape Town for R3,000 (about $160 USD) and receives a receipt but not a proper tax invoice. She also stays at a lodge that adds a 1% tourism levy to her room bill, which she notices only at checkout. On her departure day from Cape Town International Airport, Emily goes to the VAT refund office to claim a refund for the jacket, but her request is denied due to missing documentation. Was it legal for the store to deny her a proper tax invoice, and is she obligated to pay the tourism levy even though she wasn't notified in advance?*

ANSWER: *Under South African tax law, a VAT refund can only be granted if the tourist presents a valid tax invoice that complies with the requirements set by the South African Revenue Service (SARS). This includes the vendor's name and VAT registration number, the VAT amount, and a description of the goods. A basic sales receipt is not sufficient. Therefore, while the store is not legally required to issue a tax invoice automatically, it must provide one upon request if it's VAT-registered. If it fails to do so, the tourist cannot legally obtain a VAT refund. As for the tourism levy, although it operates under a voluntary system for businesses (administered by TOMSA), once a participating establishment chooses to collect it, they are expected to clearly disclose this to guests. However, there is no legal obligation for advance written notice to the traveler. If it was charged in accordance with the establishment's standard practice, and the business is registered with TOMSA, the charge is legally enforceable—even if it was only itemized at checkout.*

CHAPTER 23

LONG-TERM STAYS

IN THIS CHAPTER

- Overview
- Long-Term Visas
- Visa Application Requirements
- General Questions
- Law of the Land Hypothetical
- Law of the Land True Story
- Takeaways

CHAPTER 23

LONG-TERM STAYS

Overview

South Africa has become an increasingly attractive destination for long-term stays, drawing individuals with its diverse landscapes, vibrant culture, and relatively affordable cost of living. Many choose to reside in the country for extended periods due to its **pleasant climate, career opportunities**, and the allure of a **lifestyle that balances modern amenities with natural beauty**. Cities like Cape Town, Johannesburg, Durban, and Pretoria are particularly popular among expatriates, each offering unique experiences—from Cape Town's scenic coastal living to Johannesburg's bustling economic environment.

South Africa offers a **relatively affordable cost of living** compared to many Western countries. For example, the average rent across the country is around R7,900 (approximately $431 USD) per month. In major cities, rental costs for a one-bedroom apartment can range between R5,000 and R15,000 ($270 and $ 810 USD) per month, depending on the location and amenities. Utilities, groceries, and transportation are also reasonably priced, contributing to the overall affordability for expatriates and long-term residents.[79] However, it's important to note that while daily expenses may be lower, private healthcare can be a significant cost.

79 https://www.expatica.com/za/moving/about/cost-of-living-in-south-africa-1167470/

South Africa's healthcare system comprises both public and private sectors. While public hospitals offer services at reduced costs, they may not meet the expectations of all expatriates. Consequently, many long-term residents opt for private healthcare, which provides higher quality services but at a higher price point. Securing a robust **health insurance plan** is advisable to cover these expenses.

Housing in South Africa is diverse, ranging from modern apartments in the heart of cities to traditional houses in rural areas. The **housing market is generally more affordable** than in many Western European countries, with prices varying depending on location. In urban areas like Johannesburg and Cape Town, rental prices are higher compared to more rural areas, where one can find a spacious house or apartment for less. Many expatriates initially prefer to rent before deciding to purchase property, especially in places where the property market is more accessible.

Transportation within South Africa varies by region. In major cities, public transportation options include buses, trains, and minibus taxis. However, the reliability and coverage of these services can be inconsistent. As a result, many long-term residents prefer to own or rent a vehicle for greater convenience and flexibility.

Language is generally **not a major barrier** for most expatriates in South Africa, especially those who speak English. English is one of the country's 11 official languages and is the **primary language of business, education, and government**, particularly in urban areas like Cape Town, Johannesburg, and Durban. Most signs, official documents, and public communication are in English, and you'll find that many South Africans are fluent or proficient in it.

However, while you can comfortably live and work in South Africa using only English, **understanding or learning local languages** like Zulu, Xhosa, or Afrikaans can greatly **enhance social integration and cultural appreciation**—especially in more rural areas or when engaging with local communities. Even basic greetings or phrases in local languages are often appreciated and seen as a sign of respect.

Thus overall, South Africa presents a compelling option for long-term residency, offering a blend of affordability, cultural richness, and natural beauty. Prospective residents should plan accordingly, particularly concerning healthcare, housing, and transportation, to ensure a smooth and enjoyable living experience.

Long-Term Visas

While South Africa is not considered a major global migration hub compared to countries like Canada, Australia, or Spain, it does attract a steady stream of long-term visitors and immigrants. South Africa is home to approximately **2.9 million international migrants**, accounting for about 4.8% of its population. According to **UN migration data** and **South Africa's Department of Home Affairs**, the country hosts over **4 million foreign-born residents**, many of whom are from neighboring African countries such as Zimbabwe, Mozambique, and Lesotho. There is also a **smaller but noticeable population of expats** from Europe, North America, and Asia, often working in sectors like finance, academia, NGOs, and tourism. However, **net migration figures are not particularly high**, and some foreigners also choose to leave after a few years due to concerns over safety, bureaucracy, or economic instability. South Africa has also seen **emigration of its own citizens**, particularly skilled workers moving to countries like the UK, Australia, or the UAE.[80]

In recent years, South Africa has introduced visa reforms aimed at attracting skilled workers and remote professionals. Notably, the **Remote Work Visa,** launched in May 2024, allows eligible foreign nationals to work remotely from South Africa for **up to three years**, provided they have a valid foreign employment contract and earn a **minimum annual income of R650,976 (approximately $36,000 USD)**. These initiatives are part of broader efforts to stimulate economic growth and address skill shortages in various sectors.[81]

80 https://www.migrationpolicy.org/article/south-africa-immigration-status-history

81 https://citizenremote.com/visas/south-africa-digital-nomad-visa

Despite these efforts, South Africa faces challenges related to immigration, including xenophobic sentiments and concerns over illegal immigration. The government has acknowledged these issues and is working on further reforms to create a more efficient and welcoming immigration system.

South Africa offers several long-term visa options that cater to a wide range of travelers, including professionals, students, retirees, family members, and entrepreneurs. These visas fall under the category of **Temporary Residence Permits** and are administered by the **Department of Home Affairs.** They include:

- **Work Visas:** These include the **General Work Visa, Critical Skills Work Visa**, and **Intra-Company Transfer Work Visa.** Each has specific requirements, such as proof of employment or qualifications.
- **Study Visas:** For individuals intending to pursue education in South Africa. Applicants must provide proof of acceptance from a recognized educational institution.
- **Retired Person's Visa:** Designed for individuals wishing to retire in South Africa. Applicants must demonstrate a minimum monthly income **of R37,000 (approximately $2,000 USD)** from a pension, annuity, or other passive income sources.
- **Relative's Visa:** For immediate family members of South African citizens or permanent residents. Applicants must provide proof of the familial relationship and financial assurance of at least **R8,500 (approximately $460 USD)** per month.
- **Business Visa:** For entrepreneurs planning to invest in or start a business in South Africa. Applicants must meet specific investment and business operation criteria.

Visa Application Requirements

To apply for a long-term visa in South Africa, applicants must meet a set of **general requirements** established by the Department of Home Affairs. These requirements apply to most categories of temporary residence permits, including work, study, retirement, business, and accompanying family visas.

All applicants must hold a **valid passport** with at least 30 days' validity beyond the intended departure date from South Africa and a minimum of two blank pages for visa endorsements. A completed and signed **application form** (Form DHA-1738) must be submitted, along with proof of the **visa application fee payment.** Additional required documents typically include a recent **passport-sized photograph,** a **medical certificate** and a **radiological report** (for certain types of visas, and depending on applicant's age), and a **police clearance certificate** from each country where the applicant has lived for 12 months or more since the age of 18. Applicants must also provide **proof of financial means** to support themselves during their stay, which could include bank statements, pension slips, or proof of income depending on the visa category. If applying for a work or business visa, **additional documents** such as employment contracts, business plans, or proof of investment capital may be required.

Applications must be lodged at a South African embassy, consulate, or a Visa Facilitation Centre (VFS Global) in the applicant's home country. Processing times can vary but typically take **between 6 to 8 weeks**.

For the most accurate and up-to-date information, visit the official Department of Home Affairs visa page at **www.dha.gov.za/index.php/immigration-services/apply-for-a-south-african-visa**, or the VFS Global South Africa portal at **https://www.vfsglobal.com/southafrica/**.

General Questions

1. ***If I want to stay in South Africa long term and work, should I apply for a work permit before arriving in the country?* Yes.** If you plan to stay in South Africa long term and work, you must apply for a work visa before arriving in the country. South African immigration law requires that foreign nationals obtain the appropriate visa outside the country; you cannot enter on a tourist visa and then change your status to a work visa from within South Africa, except under rare circumstances. Applications must be submitted through the South African embassy or consulate in your home country, or through an authorized Visa Facilitation Centre such as VFS Global.

2. ***I am American. Can I retire to South Africa?* Yes.** As an American, you can retire to South Africa by applying for a **retired person visa**, which allows foreign nationals to live in the country without working, either temporarily or permanently. To qualify, you must demonstrate a guaranteed monthly income of at least R37,000 (about $2,000 USD) from pensions, retirement funds, or other passive income sources. The visa application must be made at a South African consulate or embassy in the U.S. before entering the country and includes requirements such as financial documentation, medical reports, and a police clearance.

Law of the Land Hypothetical

HYPOTHETICAL: *Lina, a 42-year-old Canadian entrepreneur, wants to open a small guesthouse (similar to a bed and breakfast) in the Garden Route region of South Africa and live in South Africa long term. She plans to invest a significant amount of her savings into the business and hopes this will qualify her for a long-term visa. Can she obtain a visa to live in South Africa if she invests in a small business?*

ANSWER: **Yes**. *Lina may be eligible for a business visa in South Africa, but the requirements are strict. To qualify, she must invest* **a minimum of R5 million (about $270,000 USD)** *into a South African business and submit a detailed business plan showing how the enterprise will contribute to the local economy and employ at least 60% South African citizens or permanent residents. She must also register the business with the* **Companies and Intellectual Property Commission (CIPC)**, *obtain a tax clearance from SARS, and submit a recommendation from the Department of Trade, Industry and Competition.*[82]

Law of the Land True Story[83]

In a crucial policy shift that impacts thousands of foreign nationals, South Africa has extended its visa concession until September 30, 2025, providing legal stay to individuals with pending long-term visa applications, appeals, or waivers. This move by the Department of Home Affairs (DHA) offers a significant reprieve to those caught in the country's immigration backlog—many of whom risked overstaying penalties despite following legal procedures.

The extension applies to all foreigners who submitted their visa applications before December 18, 2024, and are currently residing in South Africa. These individuals are now permitted to remain legally in the country while awaiting outcomes. Moreover, they can leave and return under certain conditions without jeopardizing their visa status. The DHA emphasized that this concession addresses severe administrative delays, which have affected even those complying fully with legal requirements.

82 https://www.ibn.co.za/south-africa/business-visa/

83 https://www.travelandtourworld.com/news/article/south-africa-grants-major-visa-concession-extension-ensuring-legal-stay-for-foreign-nationals-until-september-2025/

This development reflects efforts by newly appointed Minister of Home Affairs, Leon Schreiber, to improve efficiency and fairness within the immigration system. Since assuming office in June 2024, Schreiber has prioritized clearing visa backlogs and implementing system upgrades. The latest extension marks a continued effort to ensure that legitimate visa applicants are not penalized by bureaucratic shortcomings.

For foreigners seeking to stay long-term—whether for work, business, study, or retirement—this extension offers much-needed clarity and legal assurance. However, all applicants are encouraged to remain informed of further policy changes, as the government continues to modernize its immigration framework in response to public pressure and administrative strain.

Takeaways

- South Africa offers an attractive cost of living, especially compared to Western countries. Living expenses are relatively affordable, however private healthcare can be a significant expense.
- The country's healthcare system is a mix of public and private services. While public healthcare is cheaper, expatriates often opt for private healthcare due to its higher quality, making it important to secure health insurance.
- South Africa offers various long-term visa options, including work, study, retirement, relative's, and business visas. These visas are essential for those who plan to stay long-term, and the Remote Work Visa, introduced in 2024, allows eligible foreign nationals to work remotely for up to three years.
- Long-term visa applications require a valid passport, proof of financial means, medical and police clearances, and other documents depending on the visa type. Processing times generally take

6-8 weeks. Applications must be submitted outside South Africa through embassies or Visa Facilitation Centres.

- Despite the country's efforts to attract skilled workers and remote professionals, South Africa faces challenges related to xenophobia and concerns over illegal immigration. The government is working on reforms to address these issues and create a more welcoming immigration system.

CHAPTER 24

CIVIL LITIGATION

IN THIS CHAPTER

- Overview
- Personal Injury Claims and Related Compensation
- How to File a Civil Claim
- Service of Documents
- Statute of Limitations
- Getting Married in South Africa
- Law of the Land Hypothetical

CHAPTER 24

CIVIL LITIGATION

Overview

Civil litigation provides a mechanism for resolving disputes, ensuring that travelers have a way to seek justice if legal issues arise while visiting another country. It helps them understand their rights and obligations under local laws, which may differ from those in their home country. The civil litigation system offers a formal process for addressing conflicts, such as contract disputes or personal injury claims, and can deter unfair practices by encouraging businesses to comply with legal standards. It also allows individuals to seek financial recourse for damages or losses and helps protect them from potential exploitation by local entities. Overall, understanding civil litigation enhances a visitor's experience and safety while traveling.

Personal Injury Claims and Related Compensation

In South Africa, personal injury claims are governed by a combination of **common law** (**delict**) and **statutory law**. Individuals who suffer harm due to the negligent or wrongful conduct of others—such as in motor vehicle accidents, medical negligence, police brutality, public space injuries, or workplace accidents—can pursue compensation. South African delictual law requires a claimant to prove conduct, wrongfulness, fault (either negligence or intent), causation, and damages in order to succeed in a claim.

One of the most significant statutory mechanisms is the **Road Accident Fund (RAF)**, which provides compensation for injuries sustained in motor vehicle accidents caused by the fault of another driver.[84] The RAF compensates victims or their dependents for medical expenses, loss of income, funeral costs, and, in cases of serious injury, general damages for pain and suffering. However, it does not cover property damage. Claims must typically be submitted **within three years** if the offending driver is known, or two years if the driver is unidentified, as in hit-and-run cases. The fund operates as a social security safety net and claimants do not need to prove the financial standing of the wrongdoer, only their negligence.

For **injuries sustained in the workplace**, employees are covered under the **Compensation for Occupational Injuries and Diseases Act (COIDA)**.[85] This statute allows workers to claim compensation from the Department of Employment and Labour's Compensation Fund without needing to prove employer fault. Compensation may include temporary or permanent disability benefits, medical treatment costs, and death benefits to dependents. Employees covered under COIDA are generally prohibited from suing their employers directly for workplace injuries.

Medical malpractice claims fall under common law and involve suing either the healthcare provider or, in public hospital cases, the relevant government entity. These claims can be complex and require proof that the medical professional or institution failed to act with the requisite standard of care, resulting in harm. When suing the state, a claimant must give notice of intention to sue within six months under the **Institution of Legal Proceedings Against Certain Organs of State Act**, with the actual claim needing to be filed **within three years** of the incident.

For other types of injuries—such as **slips and falls** in public places, **dog bites**, or **injuries caused by defective products**—common law delict principles apply. These claims require the injured party to demonstrate that the defendant acted wrongfully and negligently, resulting in harm. In cases involving state entities, such as police brutality or unlawful

84 https://www.raf.co.za/Pages/Default.aspx

85 https://www.labour.gov.za

arrest, constitutional and delictual principles may overlap, and the same six-month notice period to the state applies.

Damages awarded in personal injury claims can include compensation for medical expenses (both past and future), loss of income, loss of support (in fatal cases), and **general damages** for pain, suffering, and loss of enjoyment of life. However, general damages are only awarded in cases where the injury is assessed as serious according to statutory or medical criteria. The time limit to bring most personal injury claims is **three years** from the date of injury, although this may be suspended in the case of minors or individuals who lack mental capacity.

Legal representation is often available on a **contingency fee basis**, meaning attorneys are paid only if the claim succeeds. This arrangement is regulated under **South Africa's Contingency Fees Act**. In some instances, individuals who cannot afford legal representation may apply for assistance from **Legal Aid South Africa,** a government-funded body providing legal services to qualifying persons.

How to File a Civil Claim

Filing a civil claim in South Africa is governed by statutory procedures outlined in the **Magistrates' Courts Act 32 of 1944** and the **Superior Courts Act 10 of 2013**, depending on the type and value of the claim. Civil disputes can be brought in one of three courts: the **Small Claims Court**, the **Magistrates' Court**, or the **High Court**. The court you approach depends on the **monetary value** of the claim and the **complexity** of the issue.

South African law allows civil claims for various disputes, including **personal injury**, **breach of contract**, **damage to property**, **unpaid debts**, **defamation**, **unlawful eviction**, and **consumer disputes**. If the claim is **under R20,000 (roughly $1,000 USD)**, the matter can typically be filed in the **Small Claims Court**, where legal representation is not allowed, and the process is simplified. Information on this process is available from the Department of Justice and Constitutional Development at **https://www.justice.gov.za/scc/scc.htm**. For more substantial claims, the **District Magistrate's Court** handles claims **up to R200,000 (about $10,500 USD)**, and the **Regional Magistrate's Court** handles claims **between R200,000 and R400,000 (around $21,000 USD)**. Claims **exceeding R400,000 (around $ 22,300 USD)** must be brought before the **High Court.**

Jurisdiction is based on the geographic location where the **cause of action occurred** or where the **defendant resides or does business.** Before initiating a civil claim, especially if the respondent is a government entity (such as a municipality, hospital, or police department), the plaintiff must comply with the **Institution of Legal Proceedings Against Certain Organs of State Act 40 of 2002.** This law requires **written notice** to be served on the relevant state department **within six months** of the cause of action.[86]

Filing the claim begins with drafting and submitting a **summons** to the court. The summons outlines the claim and is accompanied by a **statement of claim** or **particulars of claim**, detailing the factual and legal basis. In Small Claims Court, the process starts with a **letter of demand**, giving the defendant 14 days to respond. If they do not comply, a summons is issued by the **Clerk of the Small Claims Court.**

For guidance, the Justice Department provides templates and information at **https://www.justice.gov.za/scc/docs.html.**

In Magistrates' and High Court claims, once the summons is issued, it must be **served by the sheriff** of the court on the defendant. The defendant typically has **10 court days** (21 days if residing outside the court's jurisdiction) to file a **notice of intention to defend.** If they do not respond, the plaintiff may request a **default judgment.** If a defense is submitted, the matter proceeds through **pleadings**, **discovery**, **pre-trial**, and potentially to **trial.**

86 https://www.gov.za/documents/institution-legal-proceedings-against-certain-organs-state-act

Service of Documents

In South Africa, the **service of legal documents** is a formal process governed by the **Rules of Court**, which ensure that all parties in a legal matter are properly informed of proceedings against them. These rules differ slightly depending on the forum (e.g., Magistrates' Court or High Court), but the principles are broadly similar and are designed to guarantee procedural fairness.

The legal rules governing service require that all initiating legal documents (such as summonses, notices of motion, or applications) must be properly served on the opposing party. This ensures that the party has knowledge of the legal action and a fair opportunity to respond. If service is not done correctly, the court may declare the process **invalid,** and the matter could be struck off the roll or postponed.

Service can be carried out in several ways, depending on the nature of the document and the circumstances of the parties. The primary method of service in South Africa is **personal service**, which means delivering the documents directly to the individual concerned. If the defendant or respondent is not available personally, the documents may be served by **affixing them to a door** at their residence or place of business, or by **handing them to a person over 16 years old** at that address who appears to be in charge. Other permitted methods include **registered post, service at a business or workplace**, and, in certain cases and with court permission, **service by publication** or **service via electronic means** such as email. Email service may only be used if the court grants leave or if it has been previously agreed upon between the parties, in line with Rule 4A of the High Court rules.[87]

The individual responsible for effecting service is generally the **sheriff of the court**, an independent official appointed under the **Sheriffs Act 90 of 1986.** Only a sheriff or deputy sheriff has the authority to serve documents in formal litigation, and they operate within assigned

87 https://lyonsbriviklaw.com/rule-4a/

geographical jurisdictions. The sheriff must act impartially and maintain a clear record of each service attempt.[88]

The process of service involves several steps. First, the plaintiff or applicant files the document with the court registrar or clerk, who then issues it (stamps and signs the summons). The document is then delivered to the sheriff, who physically takes it to the address provided for the respondent or defendant.

Proof of service is documented formally through the **return of service**, which is an affidavit signed by the sheriff detailing how, when, and to whom the document was served. This return must be filed with the court as part of the court record. The return of service serves as conclusive evidence that the legal document was properly served, and it is critical for ensuring that subsequent steps in the legal process—such as obtaining default judgment—can proceed lawfully.

Statute of Limitations

In South Africa, the statute of limitations—referred to in local law as **prescription**—governs the time limits within which a person must initiate legal proceedings for civil claims. These rules are primarily set out in the **Prescription Act 68 of 1969**, which outlines different periods of prescription for different types of claims and provides conditions under which prescription can be interrupted, suspended, or extended.

For most **ordinary civil claims**, such as those based on **contract** or **delict** (South Africa's equivalent of tort), the standard prescription period is **three years**. This means a plaintiff has three years from the date the debt becomes due to issue a summons or otherwise formally initiate proceedings. The three-year rule covers claims for **personal injury**, **property damage**, **breach of contract**, and **unjust enrichment**, among others.

88 https://www.sheriffs.org.za

Some types of claims, however, have different prescription periods. For example:

- **Debt secured by mortgage bond:** 30 years.
- **Judgments of a court:** 30 years.
- **Tax debts to SARS:** 30 years.
- **Claims for recovery of land:** 15 years.
- **Unlawful arrest or police brutality claims against the state:** While these are subject to the standard 3-year period, they also fall under the **Institution of Legal Proceedings Against Certain Organs of State Act 40 of 2002**, which requires that **written notice** be given to the relevant state organ **within 6 months** of the incident.[89]

The prescription period begins on the date when the claimant becomes aware of the facts giving rise to the debt, or when they ought reasonably to have become aware of them. This "knowledge requirement" allows for some flexibility, especially in cases involving **latent injuries**, **medical malpractice**, or **fraud**, where the harm may not be immediately discoverable.

Several **factors can delay** (**suspend**) or **interrupt** prescription. According to sections 12 and 13 of the **Prescription Act**, prescription is suspended if the debtor is outside the Republic; if the creditor is a minor; mentally ill, or under curatorship; if the debtor is a member of Parliament or the Executive during the term of their office; and during periods of arbitration.

Prescription is **interrupted** if the debtor acknowledges liability in writing or makes a payment toward the debt. It is also interrupted by the service of a **summons or legal process** on the debtor. If a claim is filed **after the prescription period has expired**, the defendant may raise a **special plea of prescription**, which typically results in the case being dismissed unless the plaintiff can successfully argue that an exception applies. The

89 https://www.gov.za/documents/institution-legal-proceedings-against-certain-organs-state-act

plea must be formally raised by the defendant as part of their defense; courts will not apply prescription ex officio (automatically).

There are **exceptions and extensions** available under certain conditions. The courts may allow a claim to proceed in the interest of justice if extraordinary circumstances exist, particularly where the delay was caused by conduct of the defendant, systemic issues (such as lack of access to legal services), or cases involving constitutional rights. However, these exceptions are not automatic and require compelling justification.

Getting Married in South Africa

South Africa is increasingly known as a wedding destination, particularly for couples seeking scenic, affordable, and legally straightforward international ceremonies. The country offers a unique combination of natural beauty, mild climate, cost-effective services, and diverse venues, making it attractive to both local and international couples. Popular wedding settings range from vineyards in the Cape Winelands, beaches along the Garden Route, and luxury safari lodges in game reserves, to historic estates, mountain retreats, and urban chic venues in cities like Cape Town and Johannesburg.

South Africa's legal framework for marriage is relatively accessible to foreign nationals. There is no residency requirement for non-citizens wishing to marry, and the process can often be completed within a few days if documents are in order. This makes it a practical option for destination weddings compared to countries that require lengthy stays or complex bureaucratic steps. The marriage is legally recognized in most other countries if properly registered and accompanied by an unabridged marriage certificate and apostille.

In addition to legal convenience, South Africa is also known for its high-quality wedding services at relatively low costs by global standards. Professional photography, catering, décor, wedding planning, and accommodation packages are often significantly less expensive than in Europe or North America. For example, a full wedding in a

Cape vineyard, including venue hire, catering, and accommodation for a small group, can cost between $5,000 and $15,000 USD, which is a fraction of the cost in countries like the U.S. or U.K.

In South Africa, marriage is governed primarily by three legal frameworks: the Marriage Act 25 of 1961, which applies to most civil and Christian religious marriages; the Recognition of Customary Marriages Act 120 of 1998, which covers unions concluded under African customary law; and the Civil Union Act 17 of 2006, which allows for same-sex or opposite-sex partnerships in the form of either a civil union or a marriage. The process is overseen by the Department of Home Affairs (DHA), which also manages the registration of all legal marriages in the country.[90]

To legally marry, both individuals must meet several requirements. The parties must be legally competent to marry, which means they must be of sound mind and capable of understanding the nature of the marriage contract. South African law sets a minimum marriage age of 18 for men and 16 for women, although this discrepancy is controversial and may be reviewed by the courts. If either party is under 18, parental or guardian consent is required, and in some instances, the consent of the Minister of Home Affairs or a High Court judge is also needed. In addition, both individuals must be unmarried, must not be closely related by blood, and must enter the marriage freely and voluntarily. If either party is already married under South African law, they may not legally marry again unless the first marriage was concluded under customary law and is legally recognized as a polygamous union under that framework.

To begin the marriage process, both partners must provide several documents, including valid identification (a South African ID book or card, or a passport for foreign nationals), proof of address, and an affidavit of current marital status. If either party has previously been married, they must submit a divorce decree or a death certificate of the former spouse. Foreign nationals must also obtain a "letter of no impediment" from their country of origin, stating they are legally free to marry.

90 https://www.dha.gov.za

South Africa does not require a marriage license in the way that some other countries do. Instead, the couple must book an appointment with either a Department of Home Affairs official or a registered marriage officer. During this appointment, the parties' identities are verified, and they must complete and sign a declaration of intention to marry (Form BI-31). In some cases, a notice of intention to marry may be posted to give the public an opportunity to raise any legal objections, although this is not always required. The marriage can take place either at a Home Affairs office or off-site if the officiant is licensed and available.

While there are no residency requirements for foreigners wishing to marry in South Africa, foreign nationals must be physically present in the country, and they are expected to provide valid visas or residence permits, along with a letter of no impediment. In marriages involving a South African and a non-citizen, Home Affairs may require additional verification to prevent marriage fraud, including interviews or document checks.

The actual ceremony can be civil or religious. Civil ceremonies are conducted by Home Affairs marriage officers or magistrates and are typically held on weekdays during business hours. Religious ceremonies must be performed by officiants who are registered under the Marriage Act or the Civil Union Act. While Christian religious marriages may be registered directly under the Marriage Act, marriages conducted under Muslim, Hindu, or traditional African rites are not automatically recognized unless they are followed by civil registration. For customary marriages, registration must occur within three months of the ceremony as required by the Recognition of Customary Marriages Act.

After the ceremony, the marriage officer completes and submits the marriage register to the Department of Home Affairs. The couple receives a handwritten marriage certificate immediately. For official purposes, such as immigration or international recognition, couples must apply separately for an unabridged marriage certificate, which includes both spouses' full details and is issued only after the marriage has been registered. This document is essential for use outside South Africa and may take six to twelve weeks to obtain. In some cases, it may also need to be apostilled by the Department of International Relations and Cooperation (DIRCO) to be valid abroad.

There is no charge for getting married at a Home Affairs office, but there is a R75 fee (approximately $4 USD) for the unabridged marriage certificate. If the couple chooses to marry at a private venue or through a private officiant, additional service fees apply, and these are determined by the officiant or the venue.

International recognition of South African marriages depends on the laws of the receiving country. However, marriages properly registered and documented in South Africa—especially those supported by an unabridged marriage certificate and apostille—are generally recognized in most jurisdictions. Couples intending to emigrate or use their marriage certificate abroad should confirm the specific document requirements with the relevant foreign embassy or consulate.

Law of the Land Hypothetical

HYPOTHETICAL: *Alex, a tourist visiting Cape Town for a two-week vacation, slips on a wet tile inside a popular shopping mall and injures his hip. There were no warning signs or barriers indicating that the floor was wet. He is taken to a private hospital where he receives treatment and is told that he will need ongoing therapy even after returning home. Alex ends up spending $3,000 USD on medical bills in South Africa and anticipates further costs once he returns home. He also misses several prepaid tours due to the injury. Before flying home, Alex considers taking legal action to recover his expenses, but he's unsure whether a foreign tourist can sue for personal injury in South Africa.*

ANSWER: *Yes. A foreign tourist like Alex can sue for personal injury in South Africa if the injury occurred within the country. South African law allows personal injury claims under the law of delict, which requires proof that the property owner owed a duty of care, breached it (e.g., by not warning about a wet floor), and that the breach caused harm. Tourists are owed the same duty of care as residents, and shopping centers are legally required to keep premises reasonably safe. Alex may claim compensation for his South African medical bills, future treatment, and lost enjoyment of his vacation, provided he can supply medical records, receipts, and possibly witness statements or photos. The time limit for filing a personal injury claim is three years from the date of the incident. He can pursue the case through a local attorney, and while practical challenges exist for pursuing the case from abroad, a strong, well-documented claim has good prospects of success.*

CHAPTER 25

OTHER THINGS TO KNOW

IN THIS CHAPTER

- Tourists and Street Hustling
- Safety Concerns and Practical Tips
- In the Event of Death
- Experiencing Financial Hardship

CHAPTER 25

OTHER THINGS TO KNOW

Tourists and Street Hustling

Street hustling in South Africa is a **noticeable feature in popular tourist areas,** especially in cities like Cape Town, Johannesburg, and Durban. These interactions often involve individuals approaching tourists to sell handmade goods such as jewelry, beadwork, or paintings, or to offer services like informal guiding, taxi rides, or unsolicited assistance. While many vendors operate honestly, some hustlers can be aggressive or persistent, making it difficult for tourists to disengage politely. The most frequented places for street hustling include the **V&A Waterfront, Long Street,** and **Greenmarket Square** in Cape Town, the **beachfront promenade** in Durban, and parts of central Johannesburg such as the **Maboneng Precinct.**

Tourists should remain alert to common scams in these areas. One widespread scam involves **individuals pretending to help at ATMs**, where they may try to steal card details or cash. Another involves **unlicensed people offering informal tours**, sometimes leading tourists to isolated locations. Vendors may also use high-pressure tactics to guilt tourists into buying **overpriced goods. Pickpocketing schemes** using distractions like fake spills are also reported. These tactics rely heavily on tourists' unfamiliarity with local norms and their tendency to trust people who seem helpful or charismatic.

Local authorities and tourism organizations have acknowledged the issue and made efforts to manage it. Police presence in major tourist zones has increased, and official tourism bodies like Cape Town Tourism offer safety tips and awareness campaigns aimed at helping visitors recognize and avoid scams. While enforcement of anti-hustling regulations can be inconsistent, tourists are encouraged to **use official services, avoid displaying valuables,** and **remain cautious when approached by strangers in public spaces.**

Safety Concerns and Practical Tips

Interacting with street hustlers in South Africa can pose safety concerns for tourists, including the risk of **scams, theft,** and **unwanted attention.** To navigate these situations safely, it's important to be aware of common tactics and adopt practical measures.

Tourists may encounter individuals posing as officials or offering unsolicited assistance, particularly in busy areas. For instance, some scammers impersonate police officers, demanding on-the-spot fines. If approached, **always request proper identification** and insist on handling any fines at a legitimate police station.

To protect yourself, **remain vigilant in crowded places, keep personal belongings secure,** and **avoid displaying valuables.** If someone offers unsolicited help, it's acceptable to **decline politely but firmly**. Being assertive and aware of your surroundings can deter potential hustlers.

Understanding local customs can also aid in these interactions. In South Africa, maintaining a friendly yet assertive demeanor is effective. If you feel uncomfortable, it's appropriate to remove yourself from the situation without engaging further.

Should you experience harassment or scams, report the incident to the South African Police Service by dialing **10111.** Additionally, many tourist areas have information centers where staff can assist and provide guidance.

In the Event of Death

If someone traveling with you dies while in South Africa, it is essential to act swiftly and sensitively while following the country's legal procedures. Your first step should be to **contact the South African Police Service** by dialing **10111.** Police officers will arrive to secure the scene, open a case file, and begin any required investigation, especially if the cause of death is unclear or appears to be unnatural. You must also arrange for a medical professional—usually from a public or private hospital—to **officially confirm the death** and **issue a medical certificate of cause of death.**

As soon as possible, **notify your home country's embassy or consulate** in South Africa. Embassy staff can guide you through the necessary local steps, help you communicate with authorities, and assist in notifying the deceased person's next of kin if you haven't already done so. They are also a key resource for navigating administrative procedures, such as obtaining documents or locating local funeral directors who can assist with burial or repatriation arrangements. While embassies cannot cover funeral or repatriation costs, they may help identify travel insurance policies or local resources that could ease the financial burden.

Once the death has been certified, the next step involves choosing **how to manage the remains.** A licensed South African funeral home must handle the transportation, embalming, cremation, or preparation of the body for repatriation. If the body is to be returned to the deceased's home country, a local undertaker will arrange for embalming, secure a removal permit, and prepare an international-standard coffin or casket. You'll need several official documents, including the **death certificate** (issued by the Department of Home Affairs), a **certificate of embalming**, a **non-infectious disease certificate,** and a **permit for the transportation of human remains.**

Repatriating a body can be complex and costly, often ranging from **$5,000 to $10,000 USD** or more depending on the destination and circumstances. Therefore, it's vital to check if the deceased held travel insurance that includes repatriation. If not, the family may need to cover all associated expenses. For cremations, the process is generally quicker and less costly, and the ashes can be transported with far fewer formalities.

Tourists should also be aware that South Africa's Department of Home Affairs must register the death, even for foreign nationals, before any transport or burial arrangements can be finalized. The local embassy can assist in coordinating with Home Affairs and ensuring that the necessary paperwork meets the legal requirements for both South Africa and the receiving country.

Experiencing Financial Hardship

Tourists in South Africa might face financial hardship for various reasons. **Exchange rate fluctuations** between the South African Rand and other currencies, such as the US dollar or Euro, can result in unexpected differences in spending power. **Unforeseen expenses** like medical emergencies, transportation issues, or natural disasters can create unplanned financial burdens. Additionally, **theft or the loss of money and travel documents** is a common issue, particularly in major cities. Over-spending on activities, food, and souvenirs can also deplete finances quickly, especially if tourists aren't familiar with local prices. Lastly, a **lack of understanding of local costs**, such as the price of accommodations, meals, and transport, can lead to overspending, particularly in tourist-heavy areas.

If a tourist runs out of money or needs financial assistance in South Africa, there are several actions they can take. The first step is to reach out to someone back home who may be able to send money via international wire services like **Western Union** or **MoneyGram**, both of which are widely available across South Africa. If the tourist has **travel insurance**, they should review their policy to see if it covers emergency expenses like lodging, meals, or transportation due to unforeseen circumstances. In such cases, contacting the insurance provider for guidance is crucial. Additionally, tourists can **contact the home country's embassy or consulate**, as they may provide emergency financial support or help with contacting family members.

If immediate financial assistance is needed, **local NGOs** and **community organizations** such as the South African Red Cross may offer temporary food, accommodation, or referrals to other services, while tourist offices in popular areas can offer advice on navigating financial troubles and connecting with reputable resources.

Understanding local costs and currency is essential for managing expenses. For example, a basic meal at a local restaurant may cost between R100 and R250 ($5 to $15 USD), budget accommodations like hostels or guesthouses range between R200 and R600 ($12 to $35 USD) per night, while public transportation is typically inexpensive, while bus fares ranging from R10 to R40 ($0.50 to $2.50) and taxis start at R30 ($1.75 USD). Budgeting effectively can help tourists avoid financial hardship.

Setting a daily spending limit based on available funds and the duration of the stay is essential. Avoiding high-cost tourist areas and exploring less popular destinations can also help lower expenses. Always use South African Rands to avoid additional fees or unfavorable exchange rates when paying with foreign currencies. Booking accommodations and transportation in advance can help secure lower rates, and tourists should also take advantage of free activities, such as visiting parks or hiking trails, which are common in South Africa.

CHAPTER 26

QUICK REFERENCE GUIDE

IN THIS CHAPTER

- Quick Chapter References to Important Topics

CHAPTER 26

QUICK REFERENCE GUIDE

Crime in South Africa

Are there particular areas I should avoid as a tourist?

Yes. There are certain areas in South Africa that tourists should avoid due to high crime rates. In **Johannesburg,** areas like Hillbrow, Yeoville, and Berea are known for violent crime and should be avoided. The central business district (CBD) is improving but remains risky after dark. Safer areas for tourists include Sandton, Rosebank, Melrose Arch, and Parkhurst. In **Cape Town**, the Cape Flats—home to neighborhoods such as Khayelitsha, Nyanga, Mitchells Plain, and Manenberg—experiences high levels of gang violence and should generally be avoided unless visiting on a guided community-led tour. **Durban** has higher-crime townships like KwaMashu, Umlazi, and Inanda, and its CBD can be unsafe at night. In **Pretoria**, Sunnyside and the CBD are also known for higher crime rates. **Standard safety precautions are essential throughout South Africa**. Avoid walking at night in unfamiliar areas, don't display valuables, use ride-hailing apps like Uber or Bolt, and keep car doors locked. Stay within well-traveled tourist zones and remain aware of your surroundings. *For more details, see Chapter 3.*

Drug Offenses

Is the possession of marijuana legal?

Yes. The private use and possession of cannabis by adults is legal in South Africa. Following a 2018 Constitutional Court ruling, adults may possess and cultivate cannabis **for personal use in private spaces.** However, public use, distribution, and buying or selling cannabis remain illegal. Tourists should be cautious, as carrying cannabis in public or across borders can still lead to arrest.

Is the possession of cocaine legal?

No. The possession, use, sale, or trafficking of cocaine is **strictly illegal** in South Africa. It is classified as a **Schedule 2 narcotic**, and violations are treated as serious criminal offenses with penalties including imprisonment. Law enforcement maintains a zero-tolerance approach to cocaine and other hard drugs. *For more details, see Chapter 4.*

Alcohol-Related Offenses

What is the legal drinking age?

The legal drinking age in South Africa is **18 years old.** It is illegal to sell alcohol to anyone under 18, and minors are not allowed to consume, purchase, or be served alcohol in public establishments.

What is the legal blood alcohol limit?

The legal blood alcohol concentration (BAC) limit for drivers in South Africa is **0.05 grams per 100 milliliters** of blood for regular drivers. For professional drivers (such as those with a professional driving permit), the limit is stricter at **0.02 grams per 100 milliliters.** Driving over these limits is a criminal offense and can result in fines, arrest, license suspension, or imprisonment. *For more details, see Chapter 5.*

Firearm & Ammunition Offenses

Can I possess a gun?

Yes. You can legally possess a firearm in South Africa if you are **at least 21 years old** (with some exceptions), a citizen or permanent resident, and have passed both a background check and a firearm competency test. Licenses are issued for specific purposes like self-defense, sport shooting, or hunting. Each firearm requires its own license, and fully automatic weapons are prohibited.

Can I possess ammunition?

Yes. Licensed firearm owners may legally possess ammunition that matches their licensed firearm. The standard limit is 200 rounds per firearm, though those with "dedicated status" (e.g., accredited hunters or sport shooters) may possess more. It is illegal to possess ammunition without a corresponding firearm license. *For more details, see Chapter 6.*

Prostitution

Is prostitution legal?

No. As of May 2025, prostitution remains **illegal** in South Africa. Both the selling and buying of sexual services are criminal offenses under current law. This includes related activities such as brothel-keeping and solicitation.

In December 2022, the South African government introduced a bill aimed at decriminalizing sex work to enhance protections for sex workers and reduce gender-based violence. However, this legislation has not yet been enacted, and the legal status of sex work remains unchanged. *For more details, see Chapter 7.*

LGBTQ

Is homosexuality legal?

Yes. Homosexuality is **fully legal** in South Africa. The country has one of the most progressive constitutions in the world regarding

LGBTQ+ rights. Since 1996, South Africa has explicitly banned discrimination based on sexual orientation. Same-sex marriage has been legal since 2006, making it the first country in Africa to recognize it. LGBTQ individuals have the right to adopt children, serve in the military, and access equal protection under the law.

Are same sex public displays of affection socially acceptable?

Yes. However, proceed **with caution.** While there are no laws prohibiting same-sex public displays of affection, social acceptance varies by location. In major urban areas like PDA between same-sex couples is generally accepted. However, in more rural areas or conservative communities, public displays of same-sex affection may attract unwanted attention or harassment. Travelers should use discretion depending on the setting, even though legal protections are in place. *For more details, see Chapter 8.*

Arrested in South Africa

Would I be entitled to bail if I'm arrested?

Yes. If you are arrested in South Africa, you are generally entitled to apply for bail. Bail is **not guaranteed**, but courts typically grant it unless the offense is serious (such as murder, rape, or organized crime) or if there's a risk you might flee or interfere with witnesses.

Will a lawyer be provided to me if I cannot afford one?

Yes. If you cannot afford a lawyer, the South African state is required to provide one. The **Legal Aid South Africa** system offers legal assistance to individuals who meet a means test (i.e., proving you cannot afford a private attorney). This service covers both criminal and civil cases and ensures that you have representation during court proceedings. You must request legal aid, and it is typically arranged at your first court appearance. *For more details, see Chapter 10.*

Helping a Friend or Relative Imprisoned in South Africa

Can I send money to a friend or family member imprisoned in South Africa?

Yes. You can send money to a friend or family member incarcerated in South Africa, however the process and accepted methods may vary depending on the specific correctional facility. Typically, funds can be deposited into an inmate's account through official channels. It's important to contact the prison directly to inquire about the approved procedures and ensure compliance with their regulations.

Can I remain in South Africa upon release from prison or jail after my sentence is complete?

Whether you can remain in South Africa after completing a prison sentence **depends on your legal status.** If you are a South African citizen or permanent resident, you can remain in the country after release. If you are a foreign national with a valid visa or residency permit, you may also be allowed to stay, depending on the terms of your documentation. However, if you are undocumented, you will likely face deportation proceedings upon release. You do have the right to legal representation and can appeal a deportation order. It is advisable to consult with an immigration lawyer or legal aid group for guidance based on your specific situation. *For more details, see Chapter 12.*

Crime Victim Assistance

Can a victim of a crime be legally compensated?

Yes. Victims of crime in South Africa can be legally compensated, but options are limited. There is no national compensation fund, but courts may order an offender to pay compensation during a criminal trial. If not, victims can pursue civil claims against the offender. Victims of road accidents may also claim through the Road Accident Fund. While proposals for a broader compensation scheme have been discussed, none have been implemented yet.

Does the South African government offer assistance for family members of homicide victims?

Yes. The South African government provides assistance to family members of homicide victims through various support services. The **Victim Empowerment Programme (VEP)**, coordinated by the Department of Social Development, offers trauma counseling, emotional support, and practical assistance to help families cope with the aftermath of violent crimes. Additionally, organizations like **Philisa Abafazi Bethu**, founded by activist Lucinda Evans, provide community-based support, including counseling and advocacy, to families affected by violence. *For more details, see Chapter 14.*

U.S. Consulate Assistance

What are the limitations to the consulate assistance I can receive while in South Africa?

Consular assistance is limited in scope, and while your embassy or consulate can provide essential support while you are in South Africa, there are clear boundaries to what they can and cannot do. Your consulate can help you if you are arrested, injured, or fall victim to a crime. They can assist in contacting your family, provide a list of local lawyers or doctors, visit you in jail, and monitor your welfare. They can also help replace a lost or stolen passport and offer guidance in emergencies such as natural disasters or civil unrest. However, they **cannot** intervene in the South African legal process to get you out of jail, pay your legal fees or fines, provide bail, act as your legal representative, or cover personal expenses like hotel or hospital bills. *For more details, see Chapter 14.*

Police

Is there an official police force?

Yes. South Africa has an official national police force known as the **South African Police Service (SAPS)**. It is the country's primary law enforcement agency, operating under the authority of the Ministry of Police. SAPS is responsible for maintaining public order, preventing and investigating crimes, and upholding the law across the country. Officers are stationed at police stations throughout all provinces and may also work in specialized units such as organized crime, narcotics, and forensics. SAPS officers wear uniforms, carry official identification, and operate under a national mandate, though policing is often decentralized to meet local needs. *For more details, see Chapter 15.*

How to Get Legal Help in South Africa

Is there a resource in South Africa to find legal representation?

Yes. In South Africa, several official and non-profit resources can help you find legal representation, whether you are a citizen, resident, or foreign visitor.

The primary government-funded resource is **Legal Aid South Africa**, which provides free legal services to individuals who cannot afford private attorneys. They assist with criminal, civil, and family matters and have offices throughout the country. If you are looking for private legal representation, you can consult the **Legal Practice Council** (LPC), which regulates attorneys and advocates in South Africa. Their website offers tools to verify credentials and locate licensed legal professionals. You can also seek help through **law clinics** operated by South African universities, which often offer low-cost or free legal services, particularly for human rights or public interest cases.

How do I find a qualified local attorney that speaks English in South Africa?

To find qualified English-speaking attorneys in South Africa, start with the **Law Society of South Africa** (**LSSA**) website at **www.lssa.org.za**, which offers a directory of attorneys based on language and location. Websites like **FindLaw South Africa** and the **Law Society of the Northern Provinces** also provide similar search features. You can also contact local bar associations like the Cape Bar or Gauteng Bar for referrals to English-speaking barristers and your embassy may offer a list of recommended attorneys. Check reviews on sites like Google Reviews or Lawyer.com to ensure the attorney has a good reputation.

For more details, see Chapter 16.

Foreign Embassies in South Africa

Where can I find a complete and updated list of all diplomatic missions in South Africa?

You can find a complete and updated list of all diplomatic missions in South Africa through the official website of the **Department of International Relations and Cooperation** (**DIRCO**) at **https://dirco.gov.za/foreign-representation-in-south-africa/**. This includes embassies, high commissions, consulates-general, consulates, and honorary consuls, along with contact information, locations, and head-of-mission names.

Where is the U.S. Embassy in South Africa located?

The United States Embassy in South Africa is located in the administrative capital of the country, **Pretoria**:

877 Pretorius Street
Arcadia, Pretoria, 0083
South Africa

Phone: +27 (12) 431-4000
Website: https://za.usembassy.gov.

For more details, see Chapter 16.

Medical Facilities & Hospitals

What is the number I can call for ambulance and fire emergencies?

In South Africa, you can call **10177** for ambulance and fire emergencies. This number connects you to public emergency medical and fire services and is available 24/7. For police emergencies, dial **10111**. You can also dial **112** from any mobile phone, and it will route you to the nearest emergency service, regardless of your network provider.

All these numbers are free to call. It's important to provide your exact location when calling to ensure a quick response.

If I am injured while on vacation in South Africa, are there hospitals that are recommended for tourists?

Yes. If you're injured while on vacation in South Africa, several private hospitals are highly recommended for tourists due to their excellent care and English-speaking staff. Leading hospital networks such as **Netcare, Mediclinic**, and **Life Healthcare** operate top facilities in major cities like Cape Town, Johannesburg, Pretoria, and Durban. These hospitals are well-equipped, internationally accredited, and commonly used by tourists and expatriates. *For more details, see Chapter 17.*

Driving in South Africa

Which side of the road do I drive on?

In South Africa, you drive on the **left-hand side** of the road.

Can I use my driver's license from my home country to drive in South Africa?

Yes. You can use your driver's license from your home country to drive, as long as it is printed in English and includes your photo and signature. If your license is not in English, you will need an **International Driving Permit** (**IDP**) along with your original license.

How old do I need to be to rent a car?

To rent a car in South Africa, you generally need to be at least **18 years old**, but most rental companies require drivers to be **at least 21** and to have held a valid license for **at least one year**. Drivers under 25 may also be subject to a young driver surcharge. *For more details, see Chapter 18.*

Nude Beaches & Clothing-Optional Resorts

Is public nudity legal on the beaches?

Public nudity is **not generally legal** on South African beaches. Nudity in public places is considered indecent exposure under South African law and can result in fines or arrest. However, there are a few **unofficial nude or clothing-optional beaches**, such as **Sandy Bay** near Cape Town, which is widely accepted as South Africa's only unofficial nude beach. While tolerated there, it's still not officially designated as legal, so discretion is advised. *For more details, see Chapter 19.*

Tourist Taxation

Is there a room tax in South Africa?

No. South Africa does not charge a specific **room tax** like some other countries. However, a **15% Value-Added Tax** (**VAT**) is included in the price of most goods and services, including hotel stays. This tax is usually already included in the advertised price, so you won't see it added on at checkout.

Is there any fee associated with leaving South Africa by air?

No. There is **no official departure or exit fee** when leaving South Africa by air. Any applicable airport taxes or fees are generally already included in the price of your airline ticket, so you won't need to pay anything extra at the airport when departing. *For more details, see Chapter 22.*

Long-Term Stays

Do I need to return to my home country to apply for a work permit in South Africa?

Depends. If you're already in South Africa on a visitor visa, you may be able to apply for a work permit without leaving the country. However, this depends on the specific circumstances and the type of visa you're applying for. Generally, it's easier to apply from your home country, but it is possible to apply for a change of status while in South Africa in some cases.

As an American, how long can I stay in South Africa without a visa?

As an American citizen, you can stay in South Africa without a visa for up to **90 days** within a 12-month period for tourism or business purposes. This applies to travelers holding valid U.S. passports. *For more details, see Chapter 23.*

In the Event of Death

What are the key considerations for family members when deciding whether to have a loved one buried locally or repatriated after a death abroad?

When deciding whether to bury a loved one locally or repatriate the remains after a death abroad, family members should consider **emotional, financial, and practical factors.** Repatriation can be expensive, involving costs like embalming and transportation, but it may hold cultural or emotional significance for the family. Local burial may be faster and simpler but could also have different legal or logistical requirements. The family should also consider time constraints, insurance coverage, and any religious or cultural preferences. *For more details, see Chapter 25.*

EMERGENCY/IMPORTANT CONTACT NUMBERS IN SOUTH AFRICA

Please consider putting some of these numbers in your phone **prior** to traveling to South Africa.

Emergency Numbers:

- **Police:** 10111
- **Fire:** 10177
- **Ambulance:** 10177

Other Useful Contacts:

- **General Emergency Services:** 112 (can be dialed from any mobile phone)
- **Tourist Police:** 0861 222 000
- **Coast Guard:** 021 421 0800 (Cape Town) or 086 142 4100 (National)
- **Roadside Assistance:** 0800 600 190 (for emergencies on major roads)

Legal Assistance:

- **South African Bar Association:** 012 322 6441 (South African Bar Council)
- **Legal Aid:** 0800 110 110 (National Legal Aid)

USEFUL ISIZULU, XHOSA, AND AFRIKAANS PHRASES

The most commonly spoken language in South Africa is **isiZulu** (commonly known as Zulu), which is spoken by about 24% of the population. It is followed by **Afrikaans** and **Xhosa**, with **English** also being widely used in urban areas, government, and business, even though it is not the most spoken at home.

Greetings

Hi/Hello

- **Zulu:** Sawubona / Sanibonani (sah-woo-boh-nah / sah-nee-boh-nah-nee)
- **Afrikaans:** Hallo / Goeie dag (hah-loh / khoo-yee-uh dakh)
- **Xhosa:** Molo / Molweni (moh-loh / mohl-weh-nee)

Good Morning

- **Zulu:** Sawubona ekuseni (sah-woo-boh-nah eh-koo-seh-nee)
- **Afrikaans:** Goeie môre (khoo-yee-uh moh-ruh)
- **Xhosa:** Molo ekuseni (moh-loh eh-koo-seh-nee)

Good Afternoon

- **Zulu:** Siyaphila ntambama (see-yah-pee-lah n-tahm-bah-mah)
- **Afrikaans:** Goeie middag (khoo-yee-uh mid-dahkh)
- **Xhosa:** Molo emini (moh-loh eh-mee-nee)

Good Night

- **Zulu:** Lala kahle (lah-lah kah-hleh)
- **Afrikaans:** Goeie nag (khoo-yee-uh nahkh)
- **Xhosa:** Ubusuku obuhle (oo-boo-soo-koo oh-boo-hleh)

Goodbye

- **Zulu:** Hamba kahle / Sala kahle (hahm-bah kah-hleh / sah-lah kah-hleh)
- **Afrikaans:** Totsiens (tot-seens)
- **Xhosa:** Hamba kakuhle / Sala kakuhle (hahm-bah kah-koo-hleh / sah-lah kah-koo-hleh)

Magic Words

Please

- **Zulu:** Ngicela (n-gee-seh-lah)
- **Afrikaans:** Asseblief (ah-suh-bleef)
- **Xhosa:** Ndicela (n-dee-cheh-lah)

Thank you

- **Zulu:** Ngiyabonga (n-gee-yah-boh-nga)
- **Afrikaans:** Dankie (dun-kee)

- **Xhosa:** Enkosi (en-koh-see)

You're welcome

- **Zulu:** Uyemukelwa / Kulungile (oo-yeh-moo-keh-lwah / koo-loo-nee-geh-leh)
- **Afrikaans:** Dis 'n plesier / Jy's welkom (dis un pleh-seer / yays vel-kom)
- **Xhosa:** Wamkelekile (wahm-keh-leh-kee-leh)

Cheers!

- **Zulu:** Phuza! (poo-zah)
- **Afrikaans:** Gesondheid! (kheh-sont-hate)
- **Xhosa:** Phakamisa iiglasi! (pah-kah-mee-sah ee-glaa-see)

Excuse me

- **Zulu:** Uxolo (oo-koh-loh)
- **Afrikaans:** Verskoon my (fer-skwohn may)
- **Xhosa:** Uxolo (oo-ksoh-loh)

Getting Around

Where is the bathroom?

- **Zulu:** Iphi icala? (ee-pee ee-kah-lah)
- **Afrikaans:** Waar is die badkamer? (fahr is dee baht-kah-mer)
- **Xhosa:** Iphi indlu yangasese? (ee-pee een-dloo yahng-ah-seh-seh)

What time is it?

- **Zulu:** Yini isikhathi? (yee-nee see-kah-teh)

- **Afrikaans:** Hoe laat is dit? (hoo laht is dit)
- **Xhosa:** Lixesha lini? (lee-kseh-sha lee-nee)

How do I get to...?

- **Zulu:** Ngifinyelela kanjani e...? (n-gee-fee-nyeh-leh-lah kahn-gah-nee eh...)
- **Afrikaans:** Hoe kom ek by...? (hoo kom ek bay...)
- **Xhosa:** Ndifikelela njani e...? (n-dee-fee-keh-leh-lah n-jah-nee eh...)

Where does this train/bus go?

- **Zulu:** Le threne/bhasi iya kuphi? (leh treh-neh / bah-see ee-yah koo-pee)
- **Afrikaans:** Waarheen gaan hierdie trein/bus? (fahr-hehn khan heer-dee trayn/bus)
- **Xhosa:** Le nqwelomafutha/inqwelo-moya iya phi? (leh n-kweh-loh-mah-foo-tah / een-kweh-loh moh-yah ee-yah pee)

Restaurant

- **Zulu:** Iresitolente (ee-reh-see-toh-lehn-teh)
- **Afrikaans:** Restaurant (res-troo-rahnt)
- **Xhosa:** Irestyu (ee-rehs-tyoo)

How much does this cost?

- **Zulu:** Kubiza malini? (koo-bee-zah mah-lee-nee)
- **Afrikaans:** Hoeveel kos dit? (hoo-feel kos dit)
- **Xhosa:** Ixabiso linqanaba lini? (ee-khah-bee-soh leen-kah-nah-bah lee-nee)

Train/metro station

- **Zulu:** Isiteshi se-threne (ee-see-teh-shee seh-treh-neh)
- **Afrikaans:** Treinstasie / Metrostasie (trayn-stah-see / meh-troh-stah-see)
- **Xhosa:** Isikhululo sikaloliwe (ee-see-khoo-loh-loh see-kah-loh-lee-weh)

Communication

Do you speak English?

- **Zulu:** Ukhuluma isiNgisi? (oo-khoo-loo-mah ee-see-neen-gee-see)
- **Afrikaans:** Praat jy Engels? (praht yay eng-uhls)
- **Xhosa:** Uthetha isiNgesi? (oo-teh-tah ee-see-ngeh-see)

I do not understand / I don't understand

- **Zulu:** Angiqondi (ah-nee-koh-ndee)
- **Afrikaans:** Ek verstaan nie (ek fer-staan nee)
- **Xhosa:** Andiqondi / Andiva (ahn-dee-kohn-dee / ahn-dee-vah)

I don't know

- **Zulu:** Angazi (ah-n-gah-zee)
- **Afrikaans:** Ek weet nie (ek veet nee)
- **Xhosa:** Andazi (ahn-dah-zee)

Emergency

Help!

- **Zulu:** Siza! (see-zah)
- **Afrikaans:** Help! (help)
- **Xhosa:** Nceda! (n-theh-dah)

Call an ambulance!

- **Zulu:** Shayela umnyango wezempilo! (shah-yeh-lah oom-nyahn-goh weh-zehm-pee-loh)
- **Afrikaans:** Bel 'n ambulans! (bel un am-boo-lahns)
- **Xhosa:** Biza i-ambulensi! (bee-zah ee-ahm-boo-lehn-see)

I need a doctor

- **Zulu:** Ngidinga udokotela (n-gee-deen-gah oo-doh-koh-teh-lah)
- **Afrikaans:** Ek het 'n dokter nodig (ek het un dok-ter noo-rikh)
- **Xhosa:** Ndifuna ugqirha (n-dee-foo-nah oo-gkree-khah)

Police

- **Zulu:** Amaphoyisa (ah-mah-poh-ee-sah)
- **Afrikaans:** Polisie (poo-lee-see)
- **Xhosa:** Amapolisa (ah-mah-poh-lee-sah)

I'm lost

- **Zulu:** Ngilahlekile (n-gee-lah-hleh-keh-lee)
- **Afrikaans:** Ek is verlore (ek is fer-loo-ruh)
- **Xhosa:** Ndilahlekile (n-dee-lah-hleh-kee-leh)

It's an emergency

- **Zulu:** Kuyiphutha yokuphuthumayo (koo-yee-poo-thah yoh-koo-poo-thoo-mah-yoh)
- **Afrikaans:** Dis 'n noodgeval (dis un noot-khah-fahl)
- **Xhosa:** Limeko engxamisekileyo (lee-meh-koh eng-khah-mee-seh-keh-lee-yoh)

GLOSSARY

ACQUITTAL: A jury verdict that a criminal defendant is not guilty, or the finding of a judge that the evidence cannot support a conviction.

ADVERSARY PROCEEDING: A lawsuit arising from a controversy that begins with filing a complaint.

AFFIDAVIT: A written statement made under oath.

APPEAL: A request made after a trial court has decided against one party in which the losing party asks a higher court to review the decision for legal error.

ARRAIGNMENT: A proceeding in which a criminal defendant is brought to court, told of the charges, and asked to plead guilty or not guilty.

BAIL: The temporary release of a person from jail when awaiting trial, on condition that a sum of money be lodged or deposited to guarantee an appearance in court.

BARRISTER: A lawyer admitted to plead at the Bar and who may try cases in superior court.

BURDEN OF PROOF: The duty to prove disputed facts.

CAUSE OF ACTION: A legal claim in a civil action.

COMPLAINT: A written statement that begins a civil lawsuit in which the plaintiff details the claims.

CONTRACT: An agreement between two or more persons to do something or to not do something.

CONVICTION: A judgment of guilt against a person charged with a crime.

CUSTOMS DUTY: A tariff or tax imposed on goods when transported across international borders.

COURT LIAISON: A person that coordinates with attorneys to perform administrative duties, such as scheduling witnesses, sharing information with law enforcement, and overseeing the reporting of cases to foreign embassies when applicable.

DAMAGES: Money that a defendant pays to a plaintiff in a civil case if the plaintiff wins.

DEFENDANT: 1) The individual against whom a civil claim is filed; 2) The individual against whom a criminal claim is filed.

FELONY: A serious crime, punishable by more than one year in prison.

MAGISTRATE: A judicial officer of a district court, who conducts initial proceedings in criminal cases, decides criminal misdemeanor cases, conducts many pretrial civil and criminal matters on behalf of district judges, and decides civil cases with the consent of the parties.

MISDEMEANOR: An offense punishable by one year or less in jail.

PLAINTIFF: A person or business that files a formal complaint with the court.

PLEA: In a criminal case, the answer of "guilty," "not guilty," or "no contest" in response to a criminal charge.

SOLICITOR: A lawyer who advises clients, represents them in lower court, and prepares cases for barristers to try in higher courts.

SOVEREIGN IMMUNITY: A legal doctrine by which the sovereign or the state (i.e. government) cannot commit a legal wrong and thus, it is immune from criminal and civil liability and cannot be sued.

STATUTE: A written law passed by a legislative body.

STATUTE OF LIMITATIONS: A statute prescribing a period of limitation to bring certain types of legal actions. If the action is not brought within that time, the person or entity (in a criminal context) is permanently barred from suing in court.

SUBPOENA: A command, issued under court authority, for a witness to appear and to give testimony.

TESTIMONY: Evidence presented orally by witnesses.

VERDICT: The decision of a judge or jury in a case.

WARRANT: Court authorization to conduct a search or to make an arrest.

ACKNOWLEDGMENTS

This book series would never have seen the light of day without the able assistance of the following people:

Kathy Adams, my paralegal for over 22 years, who is the "Best" I've ever worked with during my entire legal career because of her amazing work ethic, organizational skills, and her ability to think outside of the box in unique and creative ways;

Ally Knez-Siddique, a professional writer, and one of my paralegals, whose eye for detail, according to her, is both a blessing and a curse;

Gino Ibanez, my former law clerk, whose exceptional research skills helped move this book along in its early stages;

Rosa Diaz Graham, my legal assistant who helped with research and word processing at the very beginning of this project;

Shelia Martin, one of my former paralegals, worked diligently on this series of books, even after taking on another job. Her organizational skills are reflected throughout;

Mindy Scarlett, my marketing and publishing "Guru"! Her creativity and vision have no boundaries!

ABOUT THE AUTHOR

Michael L. Moore practices in Orlando, Florida, the city where he spent his formative years. He credits the trauma of having his brother murdered when he was only 10 years old, as the catalyst that drew him into the practice of law.

Moore attended Florida State University, where he was a member of the FSU debate team. Upon graduating, he was awarded a full scholarship to attend the University of Tennessee College of Law, where he was elected President of the Student Bar Association. He further honed his advocacy and public speaking skills by participating in 'moot court' competitions.

After clerking at the Tennessee Attorney General's office while in law school, Moore moved back to Orlando, Florida, to work at the State Attorney's Office as a prosecutor, and where he was fortunate enough to meet the young lady that would eventually become his wife. Moore moved on to working for private law firms, both local and national, and eventually established his own law firm in 1999. He continues to make Orlando his home base.

It was the murder of a close friend and client in Jamaica that caused Moore to realize that books on laws in other countries were few and far between, and he was inspired to create Law of the Land Publishing. Moore launched Law of the Land Publishing to provide a series of guidebooks and a membership site for tourists and business travelers to stay up to date on the laws in each country they travel to, as well as having access to assistance if they run into legal issues.

“My vision is to educate people on what their legal rights are, and how they can access legal assistance, no matter where they have to travel to in the world,” said Moore. “As Americans, we have a right to due process, but in some countries, you don’t even have the right to access a square meal when incarcerated. My goal is to provide the information needed to stay out of trouble, as well as having access to assistance if trouble finds you.”

www.ingramcontent.com/pod-product-compliance
Lightning Source LLC
Chambersburg PA
CBHW071432230926
51846CB00001B/196